Basic Weight Training
for Men & Women

FOURTH EDITION

Thomas D. Fahey
California State University

MAYFIELD PUBLISHING COMPANY
Mountain View, California
London • Toronto

To my father, the Old Carioca

Library of Congress Cataloging-in-Publication Data

Fahey, Thomas D. (Thomas Davin) 1947–
    Basic weight training for men & women / Thomas D. Fahey. — 4th ed.
       p. cm.
    Includes bibliographical references (p.) and index.
    ISBN 0-7674-1203-6
    1. Weight training.   I. Title.   II. Title: Weight training for men & women.
GV546.F25   1999   99-22762
613.7' 13 — dc21   CIP

Manufactured in the United States of America
10   9   8   7   6   5   4   3

Mayfield Publishing Company
1280 Villa Street
Mountain View, CA 94041

Sponsoring editor, Michele Sordi; production editor, Linda Ward; manuscript editor, Margaret Moore; design manager, Susan Breitbard; text designer, Terri Wright; art manager, Robin Mouat; illustrators, Raychel Ciemma, Robin Mouat, and Electronic Illustrators Group; cover designer, Diana Coe; photo researcher, Brian Pecko; manufacturing manager, Randy Hurst. The text was set in 11/12 Bembo by ColorType and printed on 50# Butte des Morts by Banta Book Group.

Cover photo: © 1998 Carl Schneider.
Photo of Taiwan weight lifter Tzu-Yau Lin on page 41, © Reuters/Corbis-Bettmann.

Contents

7   Developing the Arms 85

8   Developing the Neck and Back 98

9 Developing the Abdominal Muscles 116

10 Developing the Lower Body 125

11 Exercises to Develop Speed and Power 142

12 Nutrition for Weight Training 156

Preface

WEIGHT TRAINING IS A WORLDWIDE OBSESSION. FROM IPANEMA TO IOWA, PEOPLE OF ALL AGES lift weights hoping to build firm, healthy-looking bodies. Sports scientists, athletes, and coaches have developed increasingly sophisticated methods for improving strength and performance through training and nutrition. Unfortunately, these concepts are sometimes difficult for the average person to grasp and to implement. *Basic Weight Training for Men and Women* is a primer on this enjoyable and beneficial activity. I've tried to furnish the most up-to-date information simply, without a lot of scientific jargon.

The fourth edition of this book reflects the many developments that have occurred in this popular activity since the publication of the first three editions. It contains the latest material on exercise requirements for healthy adults based on the *Surgeon General's Report on Physical Activity and Health* (1996) and the recommendations of the American College of Sports Medicine (1998). Compared to fitness recommendations of the past, these new guidelines are revolutionary. I have also included information about the controversy regarding the optimum number of sets and repetitions for gaining strength. Many experts are recommending that beginners do far fewer sets of exercises. If this proves to be effective, more people will be able to reap the benefits of weight training with far less effort. This edition presents the latest information on the physiology of strength, popular supplements, such as DHEA, androstenedione, and creatine monohydrate, the effects of weight training on health, the effects of resistance exercise during aging, and updates on popular equipment and training methods. This edition contains exciting information on developing power and speed, norm tables for strength and body composition, strength-training programs for people interested in different sports, and anatomical drawings to help you determine the muscles you work during exercise. Finally, a detailed and updated bibliography lists the latest research studies on strength, weight training, and sports nutrition.

Organization

Chapters 1 through 5 present the basic principles of weight training — the practical and scientific basis of the activity. I've tried to translate the latest information from the sports-medicine literature in a manner that will be clear to the average person. Chapters 6 through 10 describe the various major exercises (using free weights, weight machines, or your own body weight) that make up almost all weight programs. Chapter 11 is unique to weight-training books. It teaches basic principles for increasing running speed and power for basic movements using techniques developed by Eastern European sports scientists and coaches. Chapter 12 presents important information from sports nutritionists on ergogenic aids and weight control, separating fact from fiction in this very controversial area. Appendix 1 illustrates the muscular system. Appendix 2 shows which exercises are important for the most popular sports and lists specific areas for the different muscular areas of the body. Appendix 3 presents procedures and norms for popular strength tests. Appendix 4 contains addresses of quality Web sites dealing with strength, fitness, and wellness. The glossary defines relevant terms in weight training, exercise physiology, and sports nutrition.

Features

Basic Weight Training for Men and Women has many features that make it unique among weight-training books. It contains the latest information from the medical, exercise physiology, and sports-medicine literature, presented in a manner that is easy to understand. Topics include the health benefits of weight training for adults of all ages, osteoporosis, anabolic steroids, sports nutrition, eating disorders, basic muscle physiology, weight control, building speed and power through plyometric and speed exercises, and body-building secrets for toning. Every exercise is described in detail and accompanied by a figure clearly showing the major muscles it develops. Safety is stressed throughout. Caution statements are included whenever a point is particularly important for preventing injury or avoiding an accident. The appendixes include detailed anatomical charts, fitness norms and testing procedures, and suggested exercises for a variety of activities. The back cover includes a workout card so that students can track their progress during the course.

Acknowledgments

Any book is the product of more than the person who wrote it. I'm indebted to the people at Mayfield Publishing, including Michele Sordi, Linda Ward, Susan Breitbard, Robin Mouat, and Brian Peck. I'm particularly indebted to the many professors, athletes, and coaches who taught me the art and science of weight training, including George Brooks, Bob Lualhati, Frank Verducci, Franklin Henry, Art Burns, John Powell, Carl Wallen, Tom Carey, Harmon Brown, Lachsen Akka, Bob Fritz, Richard Marks, Dick Trimmer, Larry Burleson, Rich Schroeder, James Wright, and Steve Hendersen.

1

Basic
Weight Training

BE HONEST WITH YOURSELF. IF YOU HAD TO APPRAISE THE REAL REASONS YOU EXERCISE, what would they be? Would preventing heart disease and bone deterioration be at the top of the list? Unless you're much different from most people, avoiding diseases is not the reason you lift weights, go to aerobics classes, run, or swim 3 or 4 days a week. Let's face it, you exercise because you want to look and feel good.

Time is a problem. Few people have enough time to spend the whole day trying to make the Olympic team. You may have to work, go to school, take care of the family, and follow other interests. Fortunately, you don't have to devote a lot of time to a fitness program to get fantastic results. The key is to choose the right activities and design a well-structured program. Weight training can be an important part of your exercise routine.

A few hours of training a week will give you a fit, healthier-looking body as well as increased strength, which will carry over into other activities. After only a few months of weight training, you will begin to feel stronger and more confident participating in other physical activities and sports — skiing, aerobics, tennis, racquetball, volleyball, or jogging. Now is the time to get started and begin reaping all the benefits that weight training can provide.

There are many ways to begin a weight-training program, ranging from setting up a home gym to joining a posh health spa. It is generally best, however, to train in a health club or class because you can receive expert instruction. Also, you can usually work out on better equipment than you can at home.

Instruction is critical. On your own, you may waste much time and effort doing poor weight-training routines and end up with little to show for it. Worse, you may develop muscle and joint problems, such as kneecap and back pain. A competent instructor can help you avoid these pitfalls. Good health clubs have qualified instructors who can set up a program tailor-made to your needs. Try to join a club that hires instructors who have had formal training in **exercise physiology** and sports sciences and who are certified by professional organizations, such as the **American College of Sports Medicine.**

If you find it difficult to stay with a program, maybe a weight-training class is the place for you. A class makes it easier to start a program—and stay with it. It gives you a place and time to train and someone to teach you about the basics of weight training. A class helps motivate you to train consistently. Because you have made a basic commitment to attend the class, you are likelier to devote the time needed to meet your goal.

If you don't want to join a club or take a class, you can set up a home gym that either substitutes for a program at the health club or supplements your weight-training class. Weight training at home is also beneficial if you have difficulty scheduling a class, if attending a spa is inconvenient, or if you don't want to spend the money for a health-club membership. A vast array of inexpensive, high-quality home-fitness products are available that can provide many benefits of a well-equipped gymnasium. To sum up, there is a way to fit weight training into almost anyone's program.

WEIGHT TRAINING AND YOUR TOTAL PHYSICAL FITNESS PROGRAM

Weight training alone is not enough to develop and maintain optimal health and fitness. You should participate in a well-rounded health-promotion program that includes proper nutrition, good health habits, and exercise for endurance, strength, and flexibility.

Proper nutrition will supply enough energy and nutrients to help you avoid or get rid of excess body fat and to prevent diseases such as osteoporosis (bone weakness) and coronary artery disease. The healthy lifestyle includes not smoking or taking dangerous drugs, handling emotional stress properly, and having good personal hygiene.

Endurance exercise is necessary to prevent coronary artery disease; strengthen the heart, lungs, and blood vessels; and improve chemical regulation within the cells. Activities such as running, **aerobics,** cycling, and skiing contribute to endurance fitness and provide an enjoyable recreational outlet while improving other components of fitness, such as muscle strength. Flexibility training helps maintain normal joint movement, which will prevent injury and future disability (particularly as you get older). Weight training, which develops muscle strength, is an important part of a general program of developing a healthy lifestyle.

Benefits of Weight Training

Weight training provides such benefits as a more attractive body, increased strength and power, improved sports performance, enhanced self-image, and a competitive outlet. With weight training, almost all people can achieve rapid gains and improve themselves.

Weight training will help you achieve that healthy look to which most of us aspire. You can lose weight and inches, get a more shapely body, and strong muscles that are difficult or impossible to get by dieting or from other forms of exercise. Weight training is the best way to develop muscle size. No other training activity can provide the large arms, big chest, rippled abdominal muscles, and powerful legs that weight training can.

Of course, weight training will not do it all. For a fit, defined body you must watch what you eat and expend plenty of calories in endurance exercise. A combination of weight training, endurance exercise, and proper diet will improve your fitness level and tone your body.

For the past 30 years, exercise experts have emphasized the importance of cardiovascular fitness. Other physical fitness factors, such as muscle strength and flexibility, were mentioned almost as an afterthought. However, as we learned more about how the body responds to exercise, it became obvious that these other factors were vital to health, wellness, and quality of life. Muscles make up over 40 percent of your body mass. You depend on them for movement and, because of their mass, they are the site of a large portion of the energy reactions (i.e., metabolic reactions) that occur in your body. Strong, well-developed muscles help you perform daily activities better and contribute to a lean, healthy-looking body. Exercises that strengthen muscles also contribute to the health of your bones.

Improved muscle and bone health with aging (see Chapter 2)   Recent research has shown that good muscle strength will help you live a longer and healthier life. Regular, life-long participation in strength training prevents muscle and nervous system degeneration that can ruin the quality of life and increase the risk of serious injury, such as hip fracture, that can prematurely shorten your life. Older people tend to lose muscle cells, and many of the remaining muscle cells become nonfunctional because the motor units lose their nerve connection. Aging also tends to make fast-twitch (i.e., fast-contracting, powerful) muscle fibers slower. Strength training helps maintain muscle mass and function, which greatly enhances quality of life and prevents life-threatening injuries.

Bone loss, a condition called **osteoporosis,** is common in people over age 45 (particularly in women after menopause). The condition leads to fractures that can be life-threatening. Although hormonal changes due to aging account for much of the bone loss, lack of bone stress due to inactivity is a contributing factor. Strength training decreases bone loss with aging.

Improved cardiovascular function   Weight training improves blood pressure regulation. For example, blood pressure increases during high-intensity upper-body exercise, such as water skiing or shoveling snow. Intense muscle contractions constrict blood vessels, which in turn raises blood pressure. The stronger you are, however, the less your blood pressure will increase. Stronger muscles don't have to work as hard to exert the same force, so they constrict blood vessels less. Every year, many people die from the effects of high blood pressure.

| CAUTION | ◆ | High blood pressure is a leading risk factor of coronary artery disease. Do not attempt to treat this problem without medical advice. |

Weight training and body fat   Scientists have known for many years that your muscle mass determines your metabolic rate — your body's energy level. The higher your muscle mass, the more calories you burn every day. Weight training helps you gain muscle, which makes it easier to control body fat.

Increased strength and power   Increased strength and power are advantages in daily life, in tasks ranging from carrying groceries to lifting suitcases at the airport. Everyday activities such as unscrewing jar tops, pushing cars, and carrying children are much easier if you are strong.

Strength training also makes muscles, tendons, and ligaments stronger and less susceptible to injury. Although this is of obvious benefit in sports, it may also protect you from injury and disability related to everyday activities. Studies have shown that people who are stronger than average are much less susceptible to back pain. (Back pain affects over 85 percent of Americans.)

Improved Sports Performance

Have you ever skied, hiked, or played tennis with someone with poor muscle strength? They tire more easily and are less effective in the activity. People with stronger muscles hit a tennis ball harder, climb more easily to the top of the mountain, and get over the edge of a ski better. Athletes in most sports have known for years that strength training improves performance. In **strength–speed sports,** such as track and field, weight training is a cornerstone of the conditioning program.

Weight training can also help you in endurance sports such as distance running and swimming. Weak people use a greater percentage of their strength than strong people do; this compromises endurance. In endurance sports, people place great emphasis on the fitness of the heart and lungs. However, success in endurance sports requires you to run or swim fast and maintain the speed, which partially depends on muscle strength. The best way to build strength for these sports is weight training.

Whether you are an athlete or a person who just likes to play sports, increased strength can make you better in the sports you enjoy. Staying in shape through sports is a lot more fun than doing boring exercise routines for the sake of health. Weight training enhances your enjoyment in sports by making you more successful and capable of handling more advanced techniques.

Enhanced Self-Image

Everyone likes to feel special and unique. Few things improve self-image more than having a lean, healthy-looking body. Few activities affect the body so quickly and positively as weight training. Weight training provides benefits that everyone can see in a short time.

People who develop fit, attractive bodies naturally feel good about themselves. Many people who take up weight training find it a good form of personal therapy and radiate self-confidence.

Competitive Outlet

Weight training can provide people with a competitive outlet. Some people use weight training to give them a competitive edge in their favorite sport. Others compete directly in weight-training activities, such as **body building** and competitive weight lifting. Even people who are only casually interested in weight training can get satisfaction from the competitive aspects of the activity. When you lift weights, you are competing against yourself for PR's (personal records). You are always trying to lift a little more weight, do a few more repetitions, or get a more fit-looking body. There is no more important competition than that which you have against yourself.

LET'S GET STARTED!

Basic information about training and exercise helps you get the most from your fitness program. You need to know basic weight-training terms and understand how weight training affects your muscles, nerves, and joints—and where to train and what clothes to wear. In the next few chapters, I will introduce you to the basics of weight training so you can get started.

2 Weight Training and Your Body

WEIGHT TRAINING AFFECTS MORE THAN YOUR MUSCLES. IT ALSO STRENGTHENS TENDONS and ligaments and improves coordination between the nervous and muscular systems. This chapter is a primer on the effects of weight training on your body.

YOUR BODY'S RESPONSES TO WEIGHT TRAINING

Skeletal muscle is highly adaptable. Overloaded muscles get stronger, while inactive muscles get weaker. You build strength by increasing the size of muscles and improving the way your nervous system transmits information to your muscles.

How Strong Can You Get?

Three factors determine your strength-gaining potential: genetics, gender, and your training program. You can't do much about the first two factors, but you can maximize your potential with a systematic training program.

Genetic potential   Your genes determine the number of muscle fibers and fiber types within each muscle, how well your nervous system coordinates muscle function, body size, and bone length. Each of these factors helps determine your strength.

The main determinant of strength is muscle size. People with more muscle fibers per muscle can increase strength more easily than others—their more numerous fibers contribute to the greater overall strength of the muscle.

Timing and coordination, partially determined by genetics, are also important aspects of strength. The force produced by the club or racquet determines the velocity of a golf or tennis ball. Few "big hitters" in golf or tennis, however, look like Olympic weight lifters. Rather, they are able to channel forces effectively through timing and coordination. These factors are often as important as muscle size for developing effective strength (i.e., strength you can use in activities other than weight training). The remarkable athletic feats of professional basketball players, Olympic high jumpers, and world-class ballet dancers are largely due to a superior neuromuscular control and faster muscle fiber types.

Body size, which is also genetically determined, governs strength as well. Larger people tend to be stronger than smaller people. However, bone length and frame size are important, too. For example, people with shorter arms and larger chests tend to have an advantage in the bench press. They don't have to push the weight as far as people with long arms and small chests. Body size can be a disadvantage when you must move your own body weight. For example, pull-ups are typically more difficult for people with larger body weights.

Gender differences   Men and women gain strength at the same rate, but men are considerably stronger than women due to their larger muscle mass. However, when strength is expressed per unit of cross-sectional area of muscle tissue, men are only 1 to 2 percent stronger than women in the upper body and about equal to women in the lower body. Because women have a greater proportion of their muscle mass in the lower body, they can gain strength more easily in the legs than in the shoulders. Men, with much muscle in their upper bodies, have much stronger shoulders than women.

COMMON QUESTIONS ABOUT WEIGHT TRAINING AND YOUR BODY

1. How long before I see changes in my body from weight training?

You will increase strength very rapidly during the early stages of a weight-training program. Most of the changes during the first 6 weeks of training are caused by learning—your nervous system improves its ability to use muscle fibers (motor units) to exert force. Changes in muscle size take longer. You will begin to see significant changes in the way your muscles look after 6 to 8 weeks of training. Early changes in your body as a result of training occur in the nervous system; changes to muscle cells tend to occur later.

2. Will weight training make my body look better?

Weight training will increase the size of your muscles, which will tend to make your body look fitter and firmer. Most people must also reduce body fat to improve the appearance of their bodies. Increasing muscle size will do little to improve appearance if you have a large layer of fat over your

(Continued)

(Continued)

muscles. There is no such thing as spot reducing (exercising a body part to reduce body fat in the area). To reduce body fat, you must eat less and burn up more calories through endurance exercise. Body fat must be lost gradually. If you try to lose weight rapidly, you will lose some of the muscle you worked so hard to get.

3. If I stop weight training, will my muscles turn to fat?

Fat and muscle are two different kinds of tissue. Muscle does not turn into fat. However, if you stop exercising, muscles will become smaller (atrophy) due to disuse. Also, you will increase body fat if you are taking in more calories than you are using. So, if you stop exercising and eat too much food, your muscles will tend to become smaller and you will increase body fat. But your muscles are not turning into fat—you are simply losing muscle mass and gaining body fat.

4. What is overtraining? Is it possible to train too hard?

Although improving any type of fitness requires hard work, it is possible to do too much exercise. Overtraining is an imbalance between training and recovery. It may occur if training sessions are too frequent, intense, or prolonged, with insufficient rest and recovery. Depending on its severity, symptoms of overtraining last anywhere from a few days to many months. A mild case is accompanied by fatigue, depressed performance, and muscle stiffness. A more serious case may involve impaired immune function (making you more susceptible to illness), depression, stress fractures, and suppression of reproductive hormones. The latter symptom is particularly distressing in women because it can lead to loss of bone density.

The symptoms of overtraining are often subtle and difficult to detect. Suspect this condition if you fail to recover adequately from a weight-training workout after several days rest. If you find that you are training hard but not improving, perhaps you are training too hard. Try changing your program or taking a couple of extra days off. Adaptation to exercise is highly individual. A program that works well for one person may be excessive for another. The best advice for selecting the optimal training program is to start with a basic workout (see page 45), then modify it gradually. If you have trouble recovering from a training program, back off a little. However, if the program seems too easy, then increase the intensity or the number of exercises.

Although most studies have shown that women don't get big muscles from weight training, empirical evidence suggests otherwise. Just look at some top women body builders. Although some have taken anabolic steroids, which may partially account for their well-developed muscles, many muscular women have not taken these drugs.

Two other factors explaining strength disparities between the sexes are male hormone levels and speed of nervous control of muscle. **Androgens** promote the growth of muscle tissue. Androgen levels in males are about six to ten times higher than those in women, so men tend to have larger muscles. Also, the male nervous system can activate muscles faster, so men tend to have more power (power is the ability to exert force rapidly).

Training program   A well-designed weight-training program that you practice systematically will increase muscle strength in almost anyone. You are ultimately in control of your training gains—if you have a good program and train regularly, you will get stronger.

MUSCLE STRUCTURE AND STRENGTH

Muscles move the skeleton. Tendons attach muscles to bones. When a muscle contracts, it shortens and pulls on the tendon, making the bone move. Stronger muscles make it much easier to move the skeleton.

Muscles are made up of individual muscle cells connected in bundles. Muscle fibers are composed of subunits called myofibrils (Figure 2–1). Myofibrils are divided into units called myofilaments (actin and myosin), which slide across each other to cause muscle contraction (Figure 2–2). The basic contractile unit of the muscle cell is the sarcomere, which is composed of actin and myosin myofilaments. One of the goals of a weight-training program is to increase the size of muscle fibers by increasing myofibrils. This process of making larger muscle fibers is called **hypertrophy.** Generally, larger muscles tend to be stronger.

Does strength training enlarge the muscle fibers—or increase their number? The bulk of evidence suggests that strength training makes muscle fibers larger (hypertrophy), not more numerous (**hyperplasia**). However, there is some proof that muscle fibers can increase in number under certain circumstances (animal studies only). Also, some extremely strong people may be born with or develop more muscle fibers than others. Generally, though, it is muscle hypertrophy that makes muscles stronger.

The Motor Unit

Muscle fibers receive the signal to contract from nerves connected to the spinal column. A motor nerve (a nerve connected to muscle fibers) links as few as one or two muscle fibers or more than 150 muscle fibers. Nerve–muscle combinations are called **motor units** (Figure 2–3). Powerful muscles, such as the quadriceps in the legs, have large motor units—each motor nerve connects to many muscle fibers. Smaller muscles, such as those found around the eye, have much smaller motor units.

The three types of motor units are fast glycolytic (FG), fast oxidative glycolytic (FOG), and slow oxidative (SO). They are subdivided according to their strength and speed of contraction, speed of nerve conduction, and resistance to fatigue. The type of motor unit chosen by the body depends on the requirements of the muscle contraction. The body

Figure 2–1 Components of skeletal muscle tissue: fasciculi, muscle fiber, myofibrils, and myofilaments.

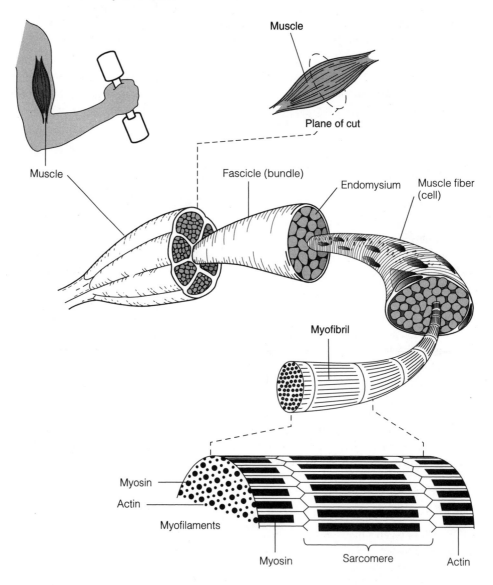

chooses FG fibers for lifting heavy weights or sprinting because they are fast and powerful. SO fibers are chosen for prolonged standing or slow walking because they are more resistant to fatigue. New fiber-typing methods subdivide fibers according to the speed of the proteins that cause the muscle fibers to contract (scientists call these proteins *myosin isoforms*).

The body exerts force by calling on one or more motor units to contract — a process known as **motor unit recruitment.** When picking up a small weight, for example, you use

Figure 2–2 The sliding-filament theory of muscle contraction. The myosin filaments pull on the actin filaments, causing the muscle fiber to shorten. The basic contractile unit of the muscle fiber is the sarcomere. The Z membrane serves as the outer boundary of the sarcomere.

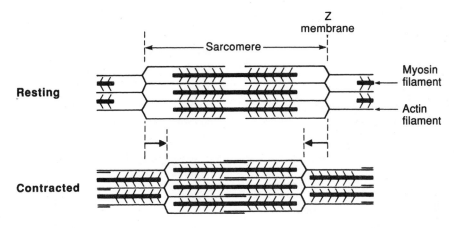

Figure 2–3 The motor unit. The motor unit is composed of a motor nerve and a number of muscle fibers.

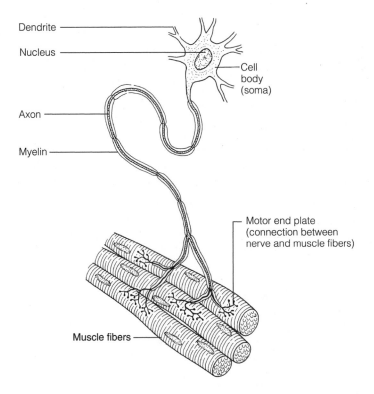

TABLE 2–1	
Changes to the Body from Weight Training	
CHANGE	EFFECT
Increased muscle mass	Tighter, firmer-looking body and stronger muscles
Increased size of fast- and slow-twitch muscle fibers	Increased muscle strength and power
Increased blood supply (high repetition program)	Increased delivery of oxygen and nutrients to the cells and increased elimination of wastes from the cells
Increased fuel storage in muscles	Increased resistance of muscles to fatigue
Ability to use more motor units during muscle contraction	Increased strength and power
Improved coordination of motor units	Increased strength and power
Increased strength of tendons, ligaments, and bone	Lower risk of injury to these tissues

few motor units to do the task. However, when picking up a large weight, you use many motor units. When a motor unit calls on its fibers to contract, all the fibers contract to their maximum capacity.

Strength increases through improved motor unit recruitment: Training with weights improves your nervous system's ability to coordinate the recruitment of muscle fibers. It is a kind of "muscle learning" and is an important way of increasing strength. Most of the changes in strength during the first weeks of weight training are due to neurological adaptations. The nervous system adapts by improving the way it stimulates motor units — it learns to call on larger motor units and better coordinates motor unit activation. Table 2–1 summarizes some ways your body improves its function through weight training.

In summary, weight training increases muscle strength by increasing the size of your muscle fibers and improving the ability to call on motor units to exert force. The first process is muscle hypertrophy, and the second process is motor unit recruitment.

WEIGHT TRAINING AND YOUR HEALTH

Weight training generally has a positive effect on health. It strengthens muscles, bones, and soft tissues, which improves the quality of life. It has small, but significant, effects on risk factors that lead to coronary artery disease.

Weight Training and the Strength of Ligaments, Tendons, Bones, and Joint Surfaces

Tendons connect muscle to bone, and **ligaments** connect bones to other bones. Cells called chondrocytes cover **joint** surfaces. These tissues have little or no blood supply, so they have a very low energy level, and they heal slowly when injured. Weight training helps strengthen the tendons, ligaments, and joint surfaces so that when you perform physical activities you're less likely to injure these structures.

Most people suffer from back pain at some time in their lives. The causes of back pain are complex. In many cases, weak, inflexible muscles in the back, legs, and abdomen cause back pain. Poor posture can also cause back pain. Weight training develops stronger, more flexible muscles. If you receive proper instruction, weight training can improve your posture by teaching you proper lifting techniques and by strengthening muscles that can take the stress off sensitive spinal nerves.

Weight Training, Weight Control, and Coronary Artery Disease

Weight training can be an important tool in a long-term weight-management program. Dieting without exercise causes decreased lean body mass (fat-free weight), negative nitrogen balance (i.e., the body loses protein), and diminished muscle strength. Weight training during dieting increases or maintains lean body mass and maintains nitrogen balance. Researchers reported improvements in strength between 17 and 22 percent in people who weight-trained during weight-loss dieting. Lean mass is the most important determinant of resting metabolic rate.

Like endurance exercise, weight training has no effect on regional fat deposition (i.e., spot reducing is ineffective). Although the improved muscle tone that results from training will usually make a particular area of the body look better, the subcutaneous adipose layer that lies over the muscles is unaffected (except as it is affected by any negative caloric balance).

Weight training may reduce the risk of coronary artery disease by helping people maintain a healthy weight, by lowering blood fats, and by decreasing blood pressure in hypertensive patients (people with high blood pressure). However, *weight training alone is not enough to prevent coronary artery disease.* It must be integrated into a healthy lifestyle program that includes endurance exercise, proper nutrition, and no smoking.

Weight training can result in explosive increases in blood pressure, so be cautious. Hypertensive patients should work with low-intensity, high-repetition training programs. They should avoid performing the Valsalva maneuver during the exercises. The Valsalva maneuver is expiring against a closed glottis (i.e., straining).

Osteoporosis

Decreased bone density, a condition called *osteoporosis,* is a serious health problem because it can lead to brittle, easily broken bones that don't heal quickly. Although the problem is usually most common in women who have reached menopause, recent evidence suggests even active women in their 20s are susceptible. The causes of decreased bone density involve an interaction of hormonal controls, diet, and mechanical stress.

CAUTION	◆	If you have reached menopause, exercise alone may not be the most appropriate treatment for preventing osteoporosis. See your doctor for proper medical advice.

Bone density is, in part, proportional to the stresses placed on the bones. Many studies show that active people have denser bones than sedentary people. If a woman's estrogen levels are normal and her dietary intake of calcium adequate, then weight training will help maintain bone density. If estrogen levels and dietary calcium are low, then weight training will be less effective in maintaining bone density. This appears to be true in adult women of any age. Once the bone growth center of bones closes, mineral content doesn't increase. The best we can do is attempt to maintain bone mineral content through weight-bearing exercise, proper nutrition, and, after menopause, possible estrogen therapy.

Weight Training and Aging

After age 30, people start to lose muscle mass. At first, you notice that you can't play sports as well as you could in high school. However, with years of inactivity and loss of strength, you may have trouble performing even the simple movements required in everyday life. Some people eventually have trouble getting out of a tub or automobile, walking up a flight of stairs, or working in the yard. When your strength is poor, it's easy to slip in the tub or hurt your back when you try to get up from a chair.

As you age, motor nerves (the nerves that turn on muscle fibers) become disconnected from individual muscle fibers. In other words, as you get older, you develop loose connections between your nerves and muscles. Muscle physiologists estimate that by age 70 in most people, 15 percent of their motor nerves become disconnected from their muscle fibers. Doing strength exercises can prevent much of this loss.

Your muscles have fast and slow motor units. Fast motor units are used to perform quick powerful movement, while slow motor units are used for slower movements, such as maintaining posture. In older muscles, the slower motor units start to take over, which makes powerful movements more difficult. Muscles become slower due to inactivity. Doing strength exercises prevents this.

Kneecap Pain

Women are particularly susceptible to kneecap pain because their wider pelvis tends to draw the kneecap to the outside (laterally) of the joint (Figure 2–4). This tends to put increased pressure on the underside of the kneecap and causes pain. However, this condition is not uncommon in men. If your kneecaps ever hurt while you are sitting down, be careful not to make the problem worse by putting excess pressure on the joint.

Figure 2–4 The Q angle is formed by the axis of the femur and the axis of the patellar ligament. A wide Q angle causes the kneecap to be pulled outward. This may irritate the underside of the kneecap and cause knee pain.

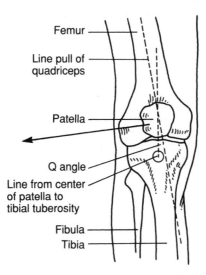

Femur

Line pull of quadriceps

Patella

Q angle

Line from center of patella to tibial tuberosity

Fibula

Tibia

Some weight-training exercises can help the problem of kneecap pain by building up the muscle on the inside of the thigh (vastus medialis). Appropriate exercises appear in Chapter 10. Also, keeping the hamstring muscles (those on the back of your thigh) as flexible as possible reduces pressure on the kneecap.

CAUTION ◆ Some weight-training exercises, such as knee extensions and full squats, may make kneecap pain worse. Check with a sports orthopedic physician or physical therapist if you are unsure which exercises are appropriate for you.

Muscle Soreness

Delayed-onset muscle soreness is an overuse injury common in people who weight-train. It usually appears 24 to 48 hours after strenuous exercise and results from tissue injury caused by muscle overload (Figure 2–5). High forces damage parts of the muscle cell responsible for contraction. Damage also causes release of calcium into the muscle. Excessive calcium is toxic to muscle. In response to the calcium, substances are released that further break down muscle cell tissue. The result is muscle soreness that peaks 24 to 72 hours after exercise. Gradually, the muscle fibers repair themselves and form proteins that protect the muscles from further damage. These protective proteins are fortified with further training but begin to disappear when you stop exercising. That's why if you take off 2 to 3 weeks from

Figure 2–5 Delayed-onset muscle soreness. Damage to the muscle results in tissue inflammation. Substances are formed that break down muscle cell tissue. Muscle soreness results. With time, the cells regenerate.

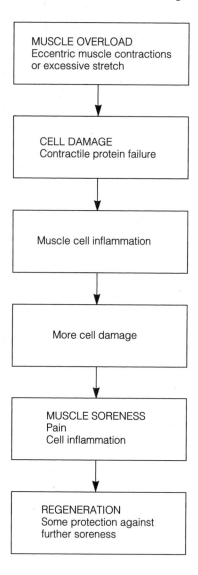

training you are more susceptible to muscle soreness. Avoid excessive muscle soreness by increasing the volume and intensity of your workout *gradually*. And, to prevent protective proteins from dissipating, avoid long layoffs from training. Stretching after exercise may also be effective in decreasing the severity of muscle soreness.

3 Basic Principles of Weight Training

THE HUMAN BODY IS A REMARKABLE ORGANISM BECAUSE IT ADAPTS TO THE PHYSICAL requirements of daily life. If you lift heavy objects regularly, then your muscles get stronger. If you seldom do any exercise, then your muscles will be small, reflecting your sedentary lifestyle.

Weight training works best when you have a plan. The plan helps you make progress in small steps that bring you closer and closer to your eventual goal. The training principles presented in this chapter are very simple but guaranteed to bring results if followed faithfully.

When you train, you are acting very much like a doctor who works to cure a disease. You administer a treatment (for example, a workout involving weight training, swimming, or running) to change the body's functioning (to improve fitness). When training with weights, you're stimulating your body to improve communications between nerves and muscles and you're getting the muscles to make more protein, which makes them stronger and improves their tone. Through training, you are compelling your body to adapt to increased demands and to improve its ability to function.

Design your training program to increase fitness and prevent injury (see discussion of stress adaptation in Chapter 4 and Figure 4–1). Every time you plan a workout, ask yourself if this exercise session is going to help your body improve its functioning. The answer won't always be yes. Sometimes rest is more appropriate than exercise, or a less intense workout is sometimes better than an exhausting one. The basic purpose of a workout is to introduce a stress you can adapt to, but not one so severe that you break down.

To get the most from your weight-training program, I recommend following thirteen principles of training. These principles are a guide to gradual and long-lasting fitness development and will lead to improved performance with the smallest risk of injury.

1. *Train the way you want your body to change.* If your main interest is general fitness, choose a well-rounded program that concentrates on the major muscle groups. Besides your weight-training routine, your program should include endurance and flexibility exercises. Weight training alone will not develop all-around physical fitness.

    Work on your weaknesses. For example, if you are a skier, having strong, flexible lower-body muscles is more important than having strong arms and shoulders. Analyze what you're doing. A well-designed program will be more effective and less time-consuming.

2. *Eat a well-balanced, high-performance diet.* During the past 20 years, sports scientists have shown that the right diet can improve performance and keep off unwanted pounds of fat. Eat a sensible, nutritious diet (one containing a balance of the basic food groups) that supplies enough calories to meet your energy needs but still allows you to control your weight. If you want to lose weight, do so gradually—lose no more than 2½ pounds per week. If you are training hard, eat more carbohydrates and fewer fats.

3. *Train all year round.* If you take off too much time from your exercise program, you will lose the gains you've made and be more susceptible to injury if you try to get back in shape rapidly. Establish a year-round program with specific goals and procedures for each period of the year—and stick to them.

    Make sure you have alternative training plans for when the weather is bad or when you don't have access to a weight room. For example, if you are on a trip, substitute calisthenic exercises—such as push-ups and sit-ups—for your regular routine. Set aside a certain part of the day for your exercise routine to ensure you will get that workout. Your exercise time is the part of the day that belongs to you alone—don't let anyone take it away.

4. *Get in shape gradually.* Training is a stress the body must overcome, so give your body time to adapt to the stress of exercise. Muscles are more susceptible to injury during the early phases of conditioning. Overzealous training, or intense conditioning when you aren't prepared for it, will lead to injury and delay progress.

    Staying in good shape all year long is much easier than trying to achieve fitness in a few months. It's much easier to apply a little pressure instead of trying to go for a crash conditioning program.

5. *Don't train when you're ill or seriously injured.* The body has problems trying to fight more than one stressor simultaneously. Training when you are sick or injured may seriously hinder your progress or even be dangerous. It is particularly important not to train when you have a fever. After an injury, you can return to intense workouts if you can answer yes to these questions:

    ◆ Can you move the injured area (joint, muscle, etc.) normally?

- Do you have normal strength and power?
- Are normal movement patterns restored (more than 90 percent recovered)?
- Are you relatively pain free?

If the answer to any of these questions is no, then let the injury heal (through a combination of **rehabilitation** and rest) or modify your program before resuming your normal workout. Dealing effectively with injuries is just as important as having a well-designed training program.

6. *Train first for volume (more repetitions) and only later for intensity (more weight or resistance).* Soft tissues, such as muscle, tendons, and ligaments, take a long time to adjust to the rigors of training. If your goal is to get as strong as possible, begin your program by doing more repetitions, not adding weight. This will prevent injury, strengthen your body gradually, and prepare it for heavy training.

    During later training sessions, when you're in shape, you can use more weight and fewer repetitions to increase strength at a faster rate. If your goal is to have good muscle tone and muscular endurance, do more repetitions instead of using more weight.

7. *Listen to your body.* Don't stick to your planned program too stubbornly if it doesn't feel right. Sometimes your body needs rest more than it needs exercise. However, if your body always tells you to rest, you won't make any progress. Most studies show that intense workouts are essential for improving fitness. If you never feel like training hard, it may be that you have a medical problem or lack motivation.

8. *Vary the **volume** and **intensity** of your workouts.* This technique is sometimes called **periodization** or **cycle training.** It allows the body to recover more fully and to train hard when intense training is called for. The principle is simple: You do a particular exercise more intensely in one workout than in another rather than training at maximum intensity for every exercise during every weight-training session.

    Although sophisticated workout cycles are most suitable to athletes, anyone can benefit from them because they help increase strength more rapidly. If your goal is to improve muscle tone and body composition (the proportion of fat and fat-free weight), you can benefit from cycle training also. Try varying the exercises in your workouts. For example, instead of doing bench presses 3 days a week, substitute incline presses 1 day. Cycle training makes working out with weights more interesting and helps you to progress faster.

9. *Don't overtrain.* This principle is difficult to stick to because it opposes the work ethic ingrained in so many of us. Think of conditioning as a long-term process. Adaptations to training happen gradually. Too much training tends to lead to overtraining and overuse injuries, not faster development of fitness. Signs of **overtraining** include fatigue, decreased

performance, irritability, and sometimes depression. Typically, an over-trained person has not recovered enough to train hard; a few days' rest is sometimes necessary to provide enough recovery to allow for more intense training.

10. *Train systematically.* Plan a proper workout schedule for the coming months, but don't be so rigid that you can't change the program to fit unforeseen circumstances. The important thing is that you have a plan so that you can comfortably and consistently improve fitness.

   A coach, training partner, and training diary will help your work-outs become more systematic. A good coach or instructor can keep you from making common mistakes and will help motivate you to meet your fitness goals. For people who need more motivation, a personal trainer — who works with you during your workout — may help you make rapid gains.

   A training partner is important for motivation and safety. This person can encourage you and **spot** (assist) you when you need help during the exercise. He or she will share the agony and ecstasy that accompanies training.

   Writing down what you hope to achieve in a training diary or workout card will help you attain your fitness goals. Use your diary to keep track of which training techniques work for you and which don't. A sample workout card is attached to the cover of this book.

11. *Train your mind.* One of the most difficult skills to acquire — but critical for attaining high levels of physical fitness — is mind control. To become physically fit or to succeed as an athlete, you must believe in yourself and your potential, have goals, and know how to achieve these goals. This requires discipline and is an ongoing process.

12. *Learn all you can about exercise.* If you know why the various compo-nents of training are important, you are much more likely to plan an intelligent, effective program. You will be less likely to jump into every training fad that comes along, and you will always be in control of your own training program. Being informed, you'll buy better and more economical sports equipment, manage many of your own athletic in-juries, and have a more efficient training routine.

13. *Keep the exercise program in its proper perspective.* Too often, the exercise program gains an unequal emphasis in a person's life. Some people think of themselves almost solely as football players, aerobic dancers, runners, triathletes, or swimmers, rather than as human beings who participate in those activities. Although exercise is important, you must also have time for other aspects of your life. Leading a well-rounded life will not diminish your chances for success and will make your training program more enjoyable.

These thirteen principles of weight training are summarized in Table 3–1.

TABLE 3–1

The Principles of Weight Training

- Train the way you want your body to change.
- Eat a well-balanced, high-performance diet.
- Train all year round.
- Get in shape gradually.
- Don't train when you're ill or seriously injured.
- Train first for volume (more repetitions) and only later for intensity (more weight or resistance).
- Listen to your body.
- Vary the volume and intensity of your workouts.
- Don't overtrain.
- Train systematically.
- Train your mind.
- Learn all you can about exercise.
- Keep the exercise program in its proper perspective.

WEIGHT TRAINING AS PART OF THE TOTAL FITNESS PROGRAM

Exercise training is an attempt to mold your body to improve it. Your body changes according to the way you stress it. If you work your muscles to exert more force than normal, the muscles get stronger. If you exercise for extended periods, your endurance improves. You can tailor your program to develop the kind of fitness you want.

Determining Your Goals

There are many weight-training exercises and programs. The right one for you depends on your goals. For example, if your goal is to have a lean, fit body, your program will be different than if you're trying to improve fitness for sports. Whatever your ultimate goal, it is best to begin the program doing 10 to 15 repetitions before trying heavy loads. Specific programs for a variety of goals appear in Appendix 2.

Developing an Attractive, Healthy-Looking Body

Developing a slim, shapely body is no easy task. Much of the problem stems from bad information and unrealistic expectations about the methods and benefits of weight training. There are several principles for people interested in developing an attractive, healthy-looking body.

The first principle is to *reduce body fat*. Weight training alone won't do it! Discussed in detail in Chapter 12, energy balance determines the control of body fat: If you consume more energy than you expend through metabolism (body chemistry) and exercise, then you gain fat; conversely, you lose fat when you expend more energy than you take in. Control body fat by eating a well-balanced diet containing adequate but not excessive calories (energy) and by doing aerobic exercise in addition to weight training.

CAUTION ◆ Don't try to improve the appearance of your body through weight training alone. Weight training should be part of a general program that includes a sensible diet and aerobic exercise.

Weight training mainly affects your muscles, which are covered by a layer of fat and skin. Increasing strength and muscle tone will do nothing if the muscles are covered by a lot of fat. Weight training *will* improve the appearance of your body if you lose fat gradually, don't develop too much loose skin, and gain muscle mass. Then the increased size of the muscles gives your body a leaner, more attractive shape.

Although having only a small effect on energy balance, weight training can improve the appearance of certain parts of the body, particularly the abdomen, to some degree. The exercises increase muscle tone, which makes the body part look tighter—but the fat will stay unless you shift the general energy balance. There is no such thing as spot reducing: You cannot lose fat in one area of the body by exercising nearby muscles.

The second principle is to build muscle size using high-intensity exercise. When combined with reduced fat, this will help tone and firm up your body. Muscles get bigger when subjected to heavy loads (that is, high muscle tension).

People who don't want to increase muscle bulk should not do very much high-intensity weight training. Instead, they should do more repetitions and use less weight. Such programs will help tone your muscles, but they develop strength more slowly than more intense ones.

CAUTION ◆ If you want to prevent excessive muscle bulk and tend to put on much muscle tissue when you weight-train, avoid low-repetition, high-resistance exercises. Instead, do more repetitions and use less weight.

The third principle of getting a great-looking body is to develop muscle definition. **Muscle definition** is the elusive property of muscles that allows their structure to be defined and seen more clearly. For example, legs look a lot better when defined muscle gives them more shape. The way to achieve muscle definition is through high-set, high-repetition workouts. However, high numbers of repetitions and sets are of limited value in improving muscle definition if you have too much body fat.

Improving Strength for Other Activities

Physical stress is necessary for improved fitness. Each sport or physical activity has specific physical demands. Skiers need strong leg muscles with plenty of endurance. Golfers need strong forearm, back, and leg muscles. Structure the weight-training routine to meet the needs of the sport.

It is also important to focus on muscles and joints commonly injured in sports. For example, many swimmers and tennis players get shoulder injuries ("rotator cuff"). Unfortunately, loosely structured weight-training programs seldom condition these muscles — until you injure them. It makes a lot more sense to precondition vulnerable joints and muscles to prevent injury.

Three major weight-training principles to practice for increasing strength for sports and daily physical activities are:

- Identify and train muscles and joints particularly important in the activity.
- Identify and train muscles and joints prone to injury in the activity.
- Maintain a good level of fitness in the major muscle groups of the body.

Developing Strength and Power

More and more people are interested in building strength for its own sake. There are weight-lifting competitions for men and women in power and Olympic lifting. Power lifting involves **maximum lifts** in the bench press, squat, and dead lift. Olympic lifting includes the clean and jerk and snatch. Many people want to improve strength for strength–speed sports, such as track and field.

The weight-training programs for people interested in improving fitness for strength–speed sports center on three types of weight-lifting exercises: presses, pulls, and multijoint lower-body exercises. Presses include the bench press, incline press, military press, seated press, push-press, jerks, and dumbbell press. Pulls include cleans, snatches, high pulls, and dead lifts. Multijoint lower-body exercises include squats, leg presses, hack squats, and rack squats.

Generally, use heavy loads (70 to 100 percent of your maximum) and a moderate number of repetitions (1 to 8 times) to gain maximum strength and power. Do supporting exercises to develop arm, back, abdominal, calf, and neck muscle strength (depending on the sport). However, presses, pulls, and multijoint lower-body exercises form the core of the program.

Strength–speed athletes have many training philosophies. Traditional programs often involved training 3 days per week, using as much weight as possible for each lift, and each workout was alike. Now, new ideas have hit the scene. Athletes and coaches have found that doing all three types of strength–speed exercises during each workout hinders recovery, leads to overtraining, and delays progress. Cycle training, in which volumes and intensities of exercises vary from workout to workout and at different times of the year, speeds up progress (Chapter 5 describes cycle training in greater detail).

WEIGHT TRAINING AS PART OF A GENERAL CONDITIONING AND WELLNESS PROGRAM

Strength training is an essential part of your physical fitness program, particularly as you get older. Fitness has many components, including cardiorespiratory endurance, muscular strength and endurance, flexibility, healthy body composition, and sports-related fitness. Each component is developed in a particular way in each sport or physical activity. For example, a person may have excellent endurance on a ski slope but poor endurance on the running track or in the swimming pool. So, to be fit for a variety of activities, you have to practice all of those activities. Regular participation in weight, flexibility, and endurance training will carry over into most of the activities of daily life and will improve your performance.

Despite the many benefits of an active lifestyle, levels of physical activity have declined in recent years and remain low for all populations of Americans. More than 60 percent of U.S. adults do not engage in recommended amounts of physical activity; 25 percent are not active at all. In the summer of 1996, the U.S. Surgeon General published *Physical Activity and Health,* a landmark report designed to reverse these trends and get Americans moving. The report summarized current knowledge about the relationship between physical activity and health; its major findings included the following:

◆ People of all ages benefit from regular physical activity.

◆ People can obtain significant health benefits by including a moderate amount of physical activity on most if not all days of the week. Through a modest increase in daily activity, most Americans can improve their health and quality of life.

◆ Additional health benefits can be gained through greater amounts of physical activity. People who can maintain a regular regimen of more vigorous or longer-duration activity are likely to obtain even greater benefits.

◆ Evidence is growing that simply becoming more physically active may be the single most important lifestyle change for promoting health and well-being.

Choosing Activities for a Balanced Physical Fitness Program

An ideal fitness program combines a physically active lifestyle with a systematic exercise program to develop and maintain physical fitness. This overall program is illustrated in the physical activity pyramid shown in Figure 3–1. If you are currently sedentary, your goal is to start at the bottom of the pyramid and gradually increase the amount of moderate-intensity physical activity in your daily life. Appropriate activities include brisk walking, climbing stairs, working in the yard, and washing your car. You don't have to exercise vigorously, but you should experience a moderate increase in your heart and breathing rates. Your activity time can be broken up into small blocks over the course of a day. The time it takes to walk to the library, climb a flight of stairs five times, and clean the house can quickly add up to 30 or more minutes of moderate activity.

The next two levels of the pyramid illustrate parts of a formal exercise program. The American College of Sports Medicine has established guidelines for creating an exercise program that will develop physical fitness (Table 3–2). A balanced program includes activities to develop all the health-related components of fitness.

◆ *Cardiorespiratory endurance* is developed by activities that involve continuous rhythmic movements of large-muscle groups. Walking, jogging, cycling,

Figure 3–1 Physical activity pyramid. Similar to the Food Guide Pyramid, this physical activity pyramid is designed to help people become more active. If you are currently sedentary, begin at the bottom of the pyramid and gradually increase the amount of moderate-intensity physical activity in your life. If you are already moderately active, begin a formal exercise program that includes cardiorespiratory endurance exercise, flexibility training, and strength training to help you develop all the health-related components of fitness.

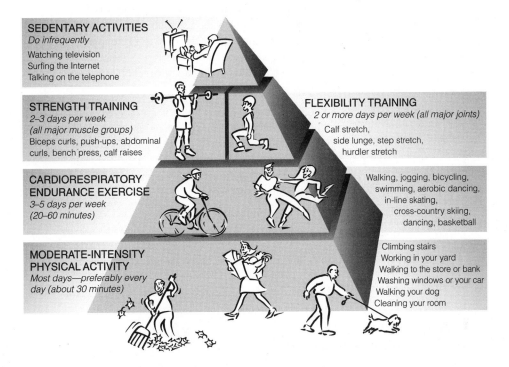

swimming, and aerobic dance (also referred to as group exercise) are all good activities for developing cardiorespiratory endurance. Choose activities that you enjoy and that are convenient. Many popular leisure activities can develop endurance, including in-line skating, dancing, and backpacking. Start-and-stop activities such as tennis, racquetball, and soccer can also develop endurance if one's skill level is sufficient to enable periods of continuous play.

- *Muscular strength and endurance,* the primary focus of this book, can be developed through resistance training — training with weights or performing calisthenic exercises such as push-ups and sit-ups.

- *Flexibility* is developed by stretching the major muscle groups regularly and with proper technique.

- *Healthy body composition* can be developed by combining a sensible diet and a program of regular exercise. Endurance exercise is best for reducing body

TABLE 3–2
Exercise Recommendations for Healthy Adults

Exercise to Develop and Maintain
Cardiorespiratory Endurance and Body Composition

Mode of activity	Any activity that uses large-muscle groups, can be maintained continuously, and is rhythmical and aerobic in nature; for example, walking-hiking, running-jogging, cycling-bicycling, cross-country skiing, group exercise (aerobic dance), rope skipping, rowing, stair climbing, swimming, skating, and endurance game activities.
Frequency of training	3–5 days per week.
Intensity of training	55/65–90 percent of maximum heart rate or 40/50–85 percent of maximum oxygen uptake reserve. The lower intensity values (55–64 percent of maximum heart rate and 40–49 percent of maximum oxygen uptake reserve) are most applicable to individuals who are quite unfit.
Duration of training	20–60 total minutes of continuous or intermittent (in sessions lasting 10 or more minutes) aerobic activity. Duration is dependent on the intensity of activity; thus, lower-intensity activity should be conducted over a longer period of time (30 minutes or more). Lower-to-moderate-intensity activity of longer duration is recommended for the nonathletic adult.

Exercise to Develop and Maintain Muscular
Strength and Endurance, Flexibility, and Body Composition

Resistance training	One set of 8–10 exercises that condition the major muscle groups should be performed 2–3 days per week. Most people should complete 8–12 repetitions of each exercise; for older and more frail people (approximately 50–60 years of age and above), 10–15 repetitions with a lighter weight may be more appropriate. Multiple-set regimens may provide greater benefits if time allows.
Flexibility training	Stretches for the major muscle groups should be performed a minimum of 2–3 days per week; at least four repetitions, held for 10–30 seconds, should be completed.

Source: American College of Sports Medicine, 1998. Position Stand: The Recommended Quantity and Quality of Exercise for Developing and Maintaining Cardiorespiratory and Muscular Fitness, and Flexibility in Healthy Adults. *Medicine and Science in Sports and Exercise* 30(6): 975–991.

fat; resistance training builds muscle mass, which helps increase metabolism (the rate of energy expenditure).

◆ *Sports-related fitness* is developed by practicing the sport. Many sports, particularly the strength–speed sports such as tennis, football, basketball, and soccer, require power and speed for optimal performance. In addition to practicing sports skills, include speed exercises and plyometric (i.e., muscle "bouncing") exercises in your program to improve performance in your sport (see Chapter 11).

Participate in as many activities as time allows, but don't get stuck in a rut or overemphasize only one component of fitness. Too many people either weight-train or run — they forget the other areas of fitness. If your goal is to develop a healthy, attractive body capable of doing many activities, you are better off participating in several types of exercise (endurance, strength, and flexibility) than concentrating on only one.

4 How Weight Training Improves Your Body

W<small>EIGHT TRAINING IS MUCH LIKE A SAVINGS ACCOUNT TO WHICH YOU ADD A SMALL AMOUNT</small> of money each week. The money from any weekly deposit will not make you rich, but the accumulated effect of many small deposits can add up to a lot of money. A single weight-training session will not improve fitness very much, but if you add the effects of months of training, improvements will be substantial.

STRESS ADAPTATION

When you subject the body to a **stress** such as exercise, it either **adapts** or breaks down. You get injured when your body can't handle the stress (see Figure 4–1). The purpose of a training program is to subject the body to a physical stress to which it can adapt—not a stress so severe it causes injury. Every time you walk into the weight room, ask yourself how the workout is helping your body to adapt and become stronger. Sometimes you will have to train harder to accelerate the rate of adaptation. At other times you will need to rest to get the most from your program.

Overload

The basis of stress adaptation is **overload,** which exposes the body to more stress than normal. The components of overload are load, repetition, rest, and frequency. Each factor affects the other. For example, if load is high, then repetitions are usually lower and rest is longer.

    Load is the intensity of exercise, the amount of **resistance,** or weight, used during the movement. Generally, the greater the load, the faster you fatigue and the longer it takes to recover. Of all the components of overload, load is probably the most important for gaining

Figure 4–1 Stress adaptation. Some exercise stress causes improved fitness, but excessive stress causes injury.

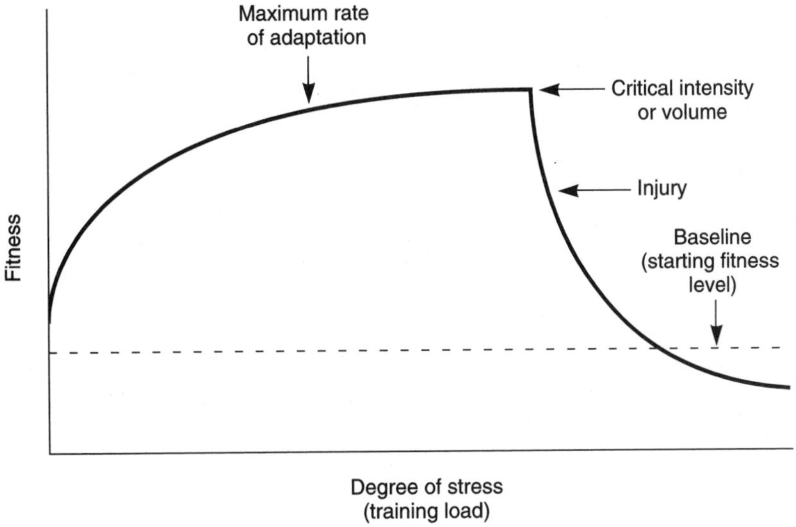

Maximum rate
of adaptation

Critical intensity
or volume

Injury

Baseline
(starting fitness
level)

Fitness

Degree of stress
(training load)

strength. High loads lead to the fastest improvements in strength and muscle size. If you are gaining more muscle mass than you want, keep the resistance down and increase repetitions.

A **repetition** is one performance of an exercise. A **set** is a group of repetitions followed by rest. Adaptation tends to happen more quickly when you do an exercise more than once. Beginners should initially use 10 to 12 repetitions and 1 to 3 sets per exercise. After 2 to 3 weeks of training, do 3 sets per exercise, with the same number of repetitions, but use more weight. Advanced routines will include between 1 and 15 repetitions, depending on the purpose of the training program. Many fitness experts currently recommend doing only 1 set of 8 to 10 exercises. They contend that the vast majority of studies show that doing 1 set of an exercise is just as effective for gaining strength as doing 2 or more sets. Studies with this finding have been conducted for as long as 6 months and have included trained and untrained people as test participants. However, other researchers and strength experts scoff at this idea and feel that you get additional benefits by including 3 or more sets of each exercise in your program. Considering this controversy, start with 1 set of each exercise, and add more sets if you find your progress slowing.

Rest, the time between sets, is vitally important for adaptation and should be applied according to the desired result. For example, a weight lifter who wants maximum strength is most concerned with load and therefore needs a considerable amount of rest between exercises. A runner is more concerned with muscular **endurance** (the ability to sustain prolonged muscular exercise), so shorter rest intervals between sets are more appropriate.

Frequency is the training sessions per week. Most people who train with weights do so three times per week, but frequency may vary between two and five times per week. People who train with weights four or five times per week typically emphasize specific muscle groups during a workout. For example, they might exercise lower-body muscle groups on Monday and Thursday and upper-body muscles on Tuesday and Saturday.

Determine frequency of training according to the desired result. Although intense training programs can improve performance in many sports, allow for proper recovery periods, or you'll get injured. More is not always better. Excessive training programs may also lead to overtraining, which will stall progress and lead to injury.

Consistency in training is also critical. You make large gains in small steps. Although overtraining is a critical problem for many people, inconsistency is the main problem for the average person. You have to do your exercise routine regularly to improve fitness.

Specificity of Training

The body adapts specifically to the stress of exercise. In other words, the adaptation to endurance exercise (e.g., distance running or swimming) is different from the adaptation to strength exercise (e.g., weight training) and power exercise (e.g., sprinting). Your training program and the exercises you choose should reflect the desired adaptation. The closer the training to the requirements of the sport, the more valuable will be the result. If you are weight training to get in shape for skiing, for example, then concentrate on lower-body exercises. If you're interested in improving your appearance, then do more varied exercises, concentrating on those parts of the body that need work.

Individual Differences

Differences in body shape, strength, physical skill, and endurance determine how fast we learn sports skills, how our body looks, and how we respond to an exercise program. Your ability to respond to any type of exercise program depends on genetics as well as the intensity of training.

Even people with naturally well-defined bodies and good health will fail to get in top shape if they don't devote enough time and effort to training. However, people without genetic gifts of fitness may find it difficult to achieve superior levels of strength and body composition — even if they "kill" themselves in the weight room.

Most of us fall somewhere in the middle between Olympic champion and total klutz. A good training program can help you develop what gifts you have and overcome your weaknesses. Even the weakest among us can get strong if the training program is intense enough and if we're patient and train consistently and correctly.

Reversibility

"If you don't use it, you'll lose it." That's an old maxim of exercise training. The purpose of weight training, or any other type of exercise, is to stress the muscles more than usual to make them stronger and larger. If you place less than normal stress on the muscles, then your muscles **atrophy** (shrink) and get weaker. In other words, gains made by training are **reversible.**

It is important to stay fit year-round. Maintaining fitness is much easier than regaining a level of conditioning you have lost. High levels of fitness and a great body call for many years of training and involve small stages of progression. Attempting to force the body to adapt rapidly will only cause injury.

TYPES OF WEIGHT-TRAINING EXERCISES

People who weight-train want at least one of three of its main effects on the body: (1) an increase in muscular strength, (2) an increase in muscular power, and (3) a change in the muscular shape. **Strength** is the ability to exert force. **Power** is work per unit of time—in other words, the ability to exert force rapidly. In most sports, power is more important than strength. Fortunately, exercises that develop strength also tend to develop power. Specific exercises to develop muscular power are discussed in Chapter 11.

Many people spend long hours developing strength in the weight room in order to increase power in sports. Tennis players, for example, often do bench presses or lat pulls so that they can serve and hit the ball harder. You lift weights more slowly than you move the racket during a tennis match, yet the strength gained during the relatively slow weight-training exercises increases power in the faster tennis movements.

There are two kinds of strength exercises: isometric (static) and isotonic (dynamic). **Isometric** exercise involves applying force without movement; **isotonic** exercise is exerting force with movement. You can do these exercises concentrically or eccentrically. A **concentric muscle contraction** occurs when the muscle applies force as it shortens. This happens during the active phase of a weight-training exercise. In an **eccentric muscle contraction,** you exert force as the muscle lengthens. For example, it may begin when you lower the weight to begin the pushing phase of the exercise.

Isometric Exercise

Isometric exercise is a static muscle contraction involving no movement. You use an immovable object, such as a fixed bar or wall, as resistance.

Although isometric exercise received considerable attention in the late 1950s, it is now less popular as a primary means of gaining strength. Isometric exercise does not increase strength through a joint's range of motion (unless practiced at various points in the range of motion); strength gains from isometrics occur only at or near the joint angle where you practiced the exercise. However, under some circumstances isometric training increases strength to some extent 20 degrees on either side of the training angle. Doing more repetitions of an isometric exercise or holding the contraction longer causes greater joint-angle strength carryover. Research studies have shown that isometric training will increase isometric force by 14 to 44 percent in 16 weeks. The total length of isometric contractions in workouts determines strength improvements. Optimal strength gains require a minimum of 15 to 20 maximum isometric contractions held for 3 to 5 seconds. Also, isometric training does not improve (and may hamper) the ability to exert force rapidly (gain power). Doing too much isometric training may lead to injury.

Weight trainers occasionally use isometrics to overcome "sticking points" in an exercise's range of motion. For example, people who have difficulty pushing weights from their chest during the bench press may do the exercise isometrically at the point where they are having the most difficulty. They may use a **power rack** for this type of isometric training (Figure 4–2).

You can also do isometric exercise without using anything for resistance. For example, you can simply tighten and release the abdominal muscles, a good way to tone and

Figure 4–2 The power rack. This device is used to help overcome "sticking points."

strengthen them. This type of exercise is particularly valuable when recovering from an injury. Examples of isometric exercises useful for strengthening the lower back and abdomen appear in Chapters 8 and 9, respectively.

   Electrical muscle stimulation (EMS) is a form of isometric exercise used by some as a substitute for active movement. The EMS machine introduces a small electrical charge into the muscle, causing it to contract. EMS can build muscle strength and is particularly valuable in injured people who are not capable of active movement (e.g., following surgery). Beware of false claims that EMS is equal or superior to weight training or aerobic exercise. It has its place but is not suitable as a primary form of physical activity.

CAUTION ◆ Electrical muscle stimulation can cause injury if applied incorrectly. If you are going to use this muscle-strengthening technique, be sure to receive proper training from your therapist or physician.

Isotonic Exercise

Isotonic exercise involves muscle contractions that result in movement. The most common and popular type of weight training, isotonic exercise may involve weight machines, barbells, dumbbells, or the body's own weight (e.g., push-ups). Isotonic techniques include constant resistance, variable resistance, eccentric loading, plyometrics, speed loading, and isokinetic exercise.

Constant resistance   The most common form of weight training, **constant-resistance** exercise uses a constant load, such as a barbell or dumbbell, throughout the range of motion. Despite the fact that you are using a constant load (the same barbell or dumbbell) throughout the exercise, the *relative* resistance of the load varies with the angle of the joint.

So, it is usually easier to move the weight at the end of the movement, where you have better leverage, than at the beginning. Maximum loading, therefore, occurs at the weakest point in the range of motion.

Variable resistance   **Variable-resistance** exercise involves special weight machines that change the load throughout the range of motion so that there is a more consistent stress on the muscles. Variable-resistance machines place more stress on the muscles at the end of the range of motion, where you have better leverage and are capable of exerting more force, than constant-resistance loads.

Many variable-resistance machines are on the market, including those made by Ariel, Hammer, Universal, Nautilus, Eagle, Marcy, and Kaiser. Sports scientists have not yet determined whether or not this form of training is superior to constant-resistance exercise. However, the machines are safe and easy to use, and they are extremely popular with many people.

Eccentric loading   As discussed earlier, **eccentric loading** occurs when the muscle lengthens while exerting force. Muscles contract eccentrically whenever you lower a weight into position prior to lifting it. This type of contraction is vital in training because it allows you to control the weight.

The active phase of most weight-training exercises (lifting the weight) is concentric. However, you can also do exercises solely eccentrically, a type of training popularly called "negatives." Eccentric loading is an effective way to gain strength and a useful supplement to concentric exercises.

Eccentric and concentric training improves both concentric and eccentric muscle strength. However, concentric training is more effective in improving concentric strength, whereas eccentric training is better for improving eccentric strength. This simple and obvious finding has important implications for training and rehabilitation. For example, hamstring strains in sprinters often occur when the hamstrings are contracting eccentrically. Optimal rehabilitation or preventive strengthening of the hamstrings is probably better accomplished through eccentric than concentric exercise. It is important to *train the body for the stresses you will encounter in your favorite sports.*

| **CAUTION** | ◆   Eccentric exercise can cause extreme muscle soreness. |

One drawback of eccentric loading is that it seems to cause more muscle soreness than other methods. The high tensions generated during this technique cause injury in the muscle that results in muscle soreness a day or two after the workout (see Chapter 2). Increase the volume and intensity of eccentric loading very gradually.

Plyometrics   **Plyometrics** involves sudden eccentric loading and stretching of muscles followed by their forceful concentric contraction. The sudden stretch stimulates receptors in the muscles and the muscles' own elasticity to react and cause a stronger contraction when they shorten.

Plyometrics are an effective way to develop power and speed. This form of exercise is particularly effective in improving communication between the muscles and the nervous system (see "Muscle Structure and Strength" in Chapter 2). Exercises to improve power and speed, including plyometrics, are discussed in Chapter 11.

| **CAUTION** | ◆ | Plyometrics can cause injury if practiced excessively. Begin with only a few repetitions of these exercises, and increase the volume and intensity very gradually. |

Speed loading (see Chapter 11)   **Speed loading** involves moving a weight as rapidly as possible in an attempt to approach the speeds used in movements such as throwing a softball or sprinting. This type of exercise may be effective in improving power (the ability to exert force rapidly). For gaining strength, weight training at ordinary speeds is superior to speed loading because speed loading prevents the muscles from creating sufficient tension to cause a training effect.

Isokinetic exercise   Also called accommodating resistance exercise, **isokinetic** exercise involves muscle contraction at a constant speed. The exerted force is resisted by an equal force from the isokinetic machine. Because you feel resistance only when you're applying force, therapists consider isokinetics safer than other forms of strength training. Isokinetic devices are used for strength training and measurement at fast speeds of movement.

Promoters of isokinetic strength-training equipment say that the machines improve power, which is the type of strength needed in most sports. Physical therapists use them for rehabilitating muscle and joint injuries. These machines are considerably more expensive than traditional weight-training equipment, so they are not as widely available.

CHAPTER

5

Getting Started:
The Basics

STARTING A NEW TYPE OF EXERCISE PROGRAM IS A LOT LIKE MOVING TO A NEW TOWN— you feel awkward, and everything is new and strange. To begin weight training, you must first make some decisions: where to train, what clothes to wear, and which exercises to do. When you know the basics, you'll feel more at ease, your program will be safer and more enjoyable, and you'll be on the path to becoming an informed fitness consumer.

MEDICAL CHECKUP

Before beginning a program, you should determine if weight training is suitable for you. Most people can exercise safely if they are in good health and follow basic training principles. However, exercise may pose a risk to health and well-being if there are pre-existing medical conditions, such as coronary artery disease. People who die suddenly from heart attacks—some of them during exercise—usually have risk factors of coronary artery disease, such as high blood pressure or cigarette smoking, that predispose them to the disease. Medical screening can help identify people who should not exercise or exercise only on a modified program. For most people, it is safer to exercise than to remain sedentary. To paraphrase the exercise scientist Per Olaf Åstrand: If you don't want to exercise, you should see a physician to determine if you can withstand the physical deterioration that occurs with the sedentary lifestyle.

Men 40 years and older and women 50 years and older, or any person with significant health problems, should get a medical examination before beginning a vigorous exercise program. If you are younger than that and in good health, there is nothing preventing you from entering a weight-training program. Health problems that need medical evaluation include high blood pressure, coronary artery disease, stroke, obesity, and musculoskeletal disorders.

It is best to choose a physician who is knowledgeable about exercise and, ideally, has training in exercise physiology or **sports medicine,** which deals with the medical problems of athletes. Local health clubs, college exercise physiology departments, and medical societies are often good sources for referrals to physicians with knowledge of sports medicine.

If you are over 40 to 50 (depending on your sex) or have significant health problems, beware of health clubs or fitness classes that offer fitness screening without proper medical supervision. Fitness evaluations by nonphysicians are not substitutes for a pretraining medical examination, and it could be dangerous to rely on them. Organizations such as the American College of Sports Medicine and the American Heart Association have established guidelines for fitness testing of adults and children (see the References section at the end of this book). Make sure your club follows these guidelines.

CHOOSING A HEALTH CLUB OR WEIGHT-TRAINING CLASS

Good health-club or college weight rooms typically have expensive and specialized weight machines that help you get the most from your program. These machines help you safely isolate and develop specific muscle groups in the chest, arms, hips, buttocks, and legs. You don't have to worry about a mountain of weights falling on your head when you miss a repetition of an exercise. Instead, if a weight is too much or not enough for you, you simply move the weight pin from one place to another in the weight stack.

Joining a health club allows you to get in some aerobic exercise, saving you a trip to the track or pool. Most clubs have aerobics classes going almost constantly. It's easy to catch a class for 40 or 50 minutes, then go to the weight room and finish your workout. If aerobics classes aren't for you, you can ride a stationary bike or train on a stair-climbing machine. Well-equipped clubs often have a running track, swimming pool, racquetball courts, or computerized rowing machines.

A club is also a great place to socialize. Many health spas have juice bars, where you can meet new friends. Socializing helps to take the drudgery out of working out.

The following guidelines can help you choose the right club. Making the wrong choice will lead to a frustrating and possibly very expensive experience.

1. *Get value for your money.*

    ◆ Be wary of signing up for a health club that does not yet exist. There have been many instances of clubs collecting money from potential members for facilities being built; then the club never opens or delays opening for many months. Research the company thoroughly before signing a "pre-opening" contract.

| CAUTION | ◆ Don't get cheated by unscrupulous health-club owners. Although most club owners are honest, the industry is plagued by "fly-by-night" operators. Check with your local Better Business Bureau or Consumer Affairs office if you think you are being treated unfairly. |

- Initiation fees and monthly dues are often negotiable. Talk to club members to get an idea of the range of possible financial arrangements. Often, initiation fees are transferable; ask about people who might want to sell their membership or check the local newspaper for this information.

- Try the club for a few months before signing a long-term contract. Health clubs make their money from people who don't use the facilities. Be particularly wary of "lifetime" memberships. The club may go out of business long before you die!

- Join a club you can afford. Many clubs charge a "prestige" fee. A more modest and less expensive club than the "Rockefeller Health Club" for $150 a month may provide you with the equipment and activities you need. Shop around!

- Don't be pressured to sign a contract on your first visit. Go home and think about the offer. Return only after all your questions have been answered and you are sure the deal is right for you.

- Make sure the contract extends your membership if you have a prolonged illness or go on vacation.

2. *The club should be convenient.*

- You probably will not attend a club very often if the club is in an inconvenient location.

- Beware of memberships that offer reduced dues if you train during "nonprime-time hours." If you can train only at 6 A.M., then a discounted early-morning membership may be advantageous. If you want to train immediately after work or school at 5:00 P.M., then pay the extra money for an unrestricted membership.

- Check out the club during the time you want to train. Verify you have easy access to the equipment and exercise classes.

3. *The club should have a well-trained staff.*

- Many universities offer degrees in exercise physiology that call for extensive study in chemistry, physiology, anatomy, nutrition, exercise physiology, sports injuries, kinesiology (study of movement), mathematics, and psychology. The best health clubs have staff members with this training. National groups, such as the American College of Sports Medicine, certify exercise leaders after they have shown adequate training and knowledge. It is no longer acceptable for health clubs to rely solely on poorly trained ex-athletes or ex-body builders for their exercise leaders. Don't join a club with a poorly trained staff!

- The club should consider your medical history before putting you on a program. This is important if you are over 40 to 50 (depending on your sex) or have any health problems.

- Beware of clubs that do exercise-tolerance tests without adequate medical supervision. Organizations such as the American Heart Association and American College of Sports Medicine have strict guidelines regarding exercise stress tests. A physician should supervise the test if you are over 40 or have significant health problems. Some clubs try to get around these regulations by doing submaximal tests. If your fitness is low, however, it is very easy for such a test to stress you maximally. Don't let clubs cut corners with your health.

- ◆ The club should have established emergency procedures.

- ◆ Choose a club that puts its members on systematic programs. Many different weight-training programs will improve strength and fitness if practiced systematically. The club should have some way of monitoring your program. Some modern health clubs are so technologically advanced that a central computer keeps track of your workout as you move from one machine to another. The next time you work out, the computer remembers what you did the time before. Although such a high-tech approach is not necessary for most people, you should make some effort to chart your progress.

4. *The club should offer amenities besides weight training.*

- ◆ If you have children, does the club offer reliable and reasonable child care? Some clubs offer fitness activities for children.

- ◆ Is there a chance to develop other types of fitness besides strength and power? Well-equipped clubs have facilities such as swimming pools; stationary bikes; rowing machines; stair machines; racquetball, volleyball, basketball, and tennis courts; and aerobics classes.

- ◆ Are you socially compatible with the membership? Different clubs attract different types of people. If you are down to earth, you may be better off avoiding a posh, pretentious health club. Some clubs cater to hard-core body builders, who can sometimes seem overbearing to the more casual weight trainer. The best way to determine the social environment is to observe the club on several occasions and talk to the members. Find a club where you will fit in.

- ◆ Many clubs have a restaurant or snack bar and a shop that sells exercise accessories, such as exercise clothing and weight belts. Although the products may be overpriced, the shop is convenient and could be an important selling point for the club.

WHAT TO WEAR

Sports clothing has come a long way since the old high-school gym suit. Modern exercise clothing is attractive, comfortable, and functional. Shorts made of elastic material, such as spandex, hug the body, supplying support. If you prefer, you can wear running shorts and a T-shirt. The main requirement for workout clothes is that they let you move easily but not be so loose they get caught in the exercise machines. Don't wear street clothes in a weight room because sweat, oil, and dirt can ruin them.

Shoes

Wear shoes that provide good lateral support, such as tennis shoes, aerobics shoes, or cross-training shoes. It is important that you wear shoes at all times to protect your feet against falling weights and people stepping on them.

If competitive weight lifting interests you, consider buying a pair of weight-lifting shoes. They provide excellent lateral support and raise your heels slightly so that you have better balance during your lifts. These shoes are available through weight-lifting and fitness magazines, such as *Powerlifting USA* or *Muscle and Fitness,* or from leading sports shoe companies, such as Adidas, Nike, and Puma. Hiking boots, which have a low heel, are a good substitute.

Weight-Lifting Belt

Serious weight trainers wear **weight-lifting belts** for back protection. Many experts feel that they support the abdominal muscles, which helps maintain proper spinal alignment when doing exercises. Although a belt may help during any exercise, it is particularly important when doing squats and pulling exercises.

| CAUTION | ◆ | Don't rely solely on a belt to protect your back. Good lifting technique and strong, flexible muscles are critical for preventing back injury. |

Belts come in a variety of colors that complement exercise clothing and look fashionable and attractive. You can buy them through exercise equipment stores or fitness magazines.

Lifting Shirts and Suits

Serious power lifters often use special clothing, such as bench shirts or stiff lifting suits, to help them lift more weight. This clothing is made of very stiff material that provides a "rebound effect" while you are doing bench presses or squats. While lifting shirts and suits are effective, they should not be used consistently during workouts. They may decondition stabilizing muscles that would normally be trained if you weren't wearing the special clothing.

Wraps

Wraps support injured joints or provide extra support. They can be made of elastic bandages, athletic tape, leather, and neoprene. Although many advanced weight trainers use wraps to support their knees, wrists, or elbows, they are unnecessary for the recreational weight trainer.

Some people use wraps to counteract knee pain during and after weight-training sessions. Although there are many causes of knee pain, one cause is the kneecap putting too much pressure on the bone underneath. Knee wraps may increase this pressure and make the pain worse. One solution is to buy a knee wrap that has a hole built in for the kneecap. The hole provides support while reducing pressure on the kneecap.

"Grip wraps" are strips of cotton webbing (such as the webbing used in karate belts) wrapped around the wrist and the weight bar; they take stress from the forearm muscles during lifts such as cleans and lat pulls. The grip is often the limiting factor in these lifts. Grip wraps allow you to use more weight during workouts so you can make faster progress.

Breast Support for Women

Although breast support is not as important in weight training as in running or volleyball, it is a good idea to wear a good sports bra whenever you exercise. The breasts can be injured if barbells press too firmly against them when weight training or if they aren't properly supported when you run. If weight training is combined with aerobics, then the need for a good sports bra becomes obvious.

A good sports bra should support the breasts in all directions, contain little elastic material, absorb moisture freely, and be easily laundered. Seams, hooks, and catches should not irritate the skin. You might consider buying a bra with an underwire for added support and a pocket to insert padding if you do exercises that could cause injury.

Gloves

Weight training can severely roughen your hands if you don't protect them. Barbells, dumbbells, and some weight machines are knurled (contain small ridges to aid in gripping), but the knurls are abrasive. Gloves may prevent your hands from getting rough and calloused. Buy gloves that fit snugly and follow the contours of the hands enough so that you don't lose too much touch. Using hand lotion after a weight workout protects the hands from roughening.

WEIGHTS AND OTHER RESISTIVE EXERCISE EQUIPMENT

Use of free weights is the most common form of resistive exercise. Other forms of resistive exercise employ weight machines, rubber hoses, water, immovable objects, or gravity (your own body weight). It is beyond the scope of this book to present exercises for all of these.

Free Weights

Free weights include barbells and dumbbells. Barbells are usually 5 to 7 feet long, with weights placed at both ends, secured by collars. The two most common types of barbells are standard and Olympic. Specialized barbells are available for doing curls (see Chapter 7), squats, and rotator-cuff exercises.

Standard barbells vary in length and weight. To get the total weight you're lifting, you must know the weight of the bar as well as that of the weight plates at the ends. In general, standard barbells weigh 15 to 30 pounds.

Olympic barbells are 7 feet long, weigh 45 pounds (20 kg), and have a rotating sleeve at each end (Figure 5–1). The finest bars are made of spring steel; these bend and recoil during heavy lifts but remain straight after the lift. Poor quality bars are often permanently bent when loaded with a lot of weight.

Figure 5–1 Olympic weight lifters such as Tzu-Yau Lin of Taiwan have utilized scientific training techniques that result in fantastic feats of human muscular strength. Photo: © Reuters/The Bettmann Archive.

Olympic weight plates have larger holes than standard plates, so can be used only with Olympic barbells. The most common weight-plate denominations are 20, 15, 10, 5, 2½, and 1¼ pounds per plate. Heavier or lighter plates are available for weight-lifting contests or leg-press machines. Rubberized plates, called bumper plates, are used to protect the floor in Olympic weight lifting because the plates are often dropped during training or competition.

Olympic bars have special markings to help you get an even grip. The middle of the bar is typically smooth, but most of the bar is knurled (roughened) to provide a good grip. Markers are also found toward the end of the bar that help you get an even handhold for wide-grip exercises, such as the snatch (an Olympic lift).

Collars are used to prevent the weights from falling off the bar. Collars weigh 5 pounds (2.5 kg) apiece. A relatively new innovation is the clip collar, which weighs very little, secures the weights tightly, and slides easily on and off the bar.

Dumbbells are much shorter than barbells and are generally held in each hand. They are constructed from various combinations of weight plates or are molded into a particular weight. Most well-equipped gyms have large racks of dumbbells, ranging in weight from 2½ pounds to well over 100 pounds.

Weight Machines

The weight room has gone "high tech." It is amazing to go to a commercial fitness show and see the incredible array of computerized exercise machines; rowing machines that allow you to compete against a computerized rower; machines that "remember" your last workout and automatically provide the right resistance for you. Are these technological marvels going to make you twice as strong, in half the time, with less work than traditional free weights? No!

TABLE 5–1
A Comparison of Free Weights and Exercise Machines

EXERCISE MACHINES

Advantages

- Safe
- Convenient
- Don't require spotters
- Provide variable resistance
- Have high-tech appeal
- Require less skill
- Make it easy to move from one exercise to the next

Disadvantages

- Expensive to buy
- Expensive to maintain
- Inappropriate for performing dynamic movements
- Offer only limited number of exercises

FREE WEIGHTS

Advantages

- Allow dynamic movements
- Develop control of weight
- Help overcome strength differences between the two sides of the body
- Allow greater variety of exercises
- Less expensive to buy and maintain

Disadvantages

- Not as safe
- Require spotters
- Require more skill
- Can cause equipment clutter
- Cause more blisters and callouses

Muscles get stronger if you make them work against resistance. You can increase strength by pushing against free weights (barbells and dumbbells), your own body weight, or sophisticated exercise machines. Table 5–1 summarizes the advantages and disadvantages of free weights and exercise machines.

Exercise machines are the preferred method of weight training by many people because they are safe, convenient, and technologically advanced. All you need to do is to set the resistance (usually done by placing a pin in the weight stack), sit down on the machine, and start exercising. You don't have to bother anyone for a spot (assistance) or worry about a weight crashing down on you. Many people can work out in a small area. Also, free weights tend to twist in your hands when you try to balance them, which can cause blisters and callouses, whereas weight machines require little or no balancing. So, beginners find the machines easier to use.

Weight machines also provide different amounts of resistance as you do the exercise — the weight is heavier as the exercise progresses. The theory behind this feature is that the stress on the muscle is more uniform as it contracts through its range of motion. It is not known whether this feature is superior to the resistance supplied by free weights.

Few skilled strength–speed athletes train on machines. Their programs center on three main exercises: presses (bench press, incline press, etc.), pulls (cleans, snatches, etc.), and squats. Explosive lifts, such as pulls, are difficult or impossible to mimic on machines.

Machines restrict you to a few movements, whereas many exercises are possible with free weights.

Popular weight machines are expensive to buy and maintain. You can buy an elementary free-weight set at a fraction of the cost. However, to equip a gym with a full array of free-weight equipment, including Olympic weights, dumbbells, and **racks,** is also very expensive. So don't base the choice between weight machines and free weights on cost alone.

Many coaches and athletes feel free-weight exercises are essential to developing explosive strength for sports. Because free weights are not on a controlled track the way machine weights are, you must control them, which probably helps to increase strength. Free weights help to overcome asymmetrical strength and let you do a greater variety of exercises. So, which is better? Because you can increase strength either way, it really boils down to personal preference.

OTHER FORMS OF RESISTIVE EXERCISE

You don't need expensive weight machines or even free weights to get a weight workout. Anything that provides resistance to your muscles can help you increase strength.

Gravity

Your own body weight provides excellent resistance for your muscles. Traditional reliable exercises such as pull-ups, push-ups, sit-ups, and dips (sometimes called calisthenics) use gravity as the resistance and require little or no equipment. The most popular calisthenic exercises are described throughout this book.

Rubber (Surgical) Tubing

Rubber tubing is an excellent and inexpensive source of resistance. You can simulate the movements of many popular free-weight and weight-machine exercises using a few dollars' worth of surgical tubing. If you need more resistance, use thicker tubing.

Water

Water has become a popular resistance medium because the risk of injury is low and it is less threatening to beginning exercisers. Water is much more viscous than air, so almost any movement becomes more difficult. Using fins on the hands and feet increases the resistance and thus the intensity of the exercise.

Other Devices

Weight-equipment manufacturers show considerable ingenuity in designing resistive exercise devices. These devices range in complexity from friction placed on a rope that is wrapped around a cylinder to complicated instruments that use variable-speed motors. The important thing to remember is that almost any equipment or technique that provides resistance to muscle contraction will increase strength — if you train systematically with it.

TABLE 5–2
Resistive Exercise Program without Equipment

Body Part	Exercise	Sets	Reps
Neck	Manual neck exercise	1–3	1 (10–20 sec)
Trapezius ("Traps")	Isometric shoulder shrugs using low bar or doorknob for resistance	1–3	1 (10–20 sec)
Deltoids	Push-ups	1–3	25
Latissimus dorsi ("Lats")	Pull-ups	1–3	5
Abdominals	Hip flexors Leg raises Crunches Sit-ups Side-bends Twists Reverse beetles	1–3	10–25
	Isometric tighteners	1–3	1 (10–40 sec)
Lower back	Spine extensions Pelvic tilts	1–3	1 (10–40 sec)
Thigh and buttocks	Squats	1–3	10–20
	Wall squats (Phantom chair)	1–3	1 (10–40 sec)
Calf	Heel raises	1–3	10–20

RESISTIVE EXERCISE WITHOUT WEIGHTS

You can increase strength without weights, using your body weight and gravity as resistance. Although these exercises will not build strength as well as weight training, they are convenient. For people interested mainly in aerobic exercise, these exercises help increase muscle mass without having to join a gym or take a class.

Table 5–2 describes a basic program you can do in your home that doesn't require any equipment (other than chairs for chair dips and a doorframe pull-up bar). Because your body weight is constant, increase the intensity of the exercise by doing more repetitions. For some exercises, you can increase resistance by changing body position or using household items to add weight to your body. For example, push-ups become more difficult if you elevate your feet by putting them on a chair. For pull-ups, add body weight by putting sandbags in your pocket. You can make sandbags by filling old socks with sand. With a little imagination, you can create a "home gym" without any equipment.

STRUCTURE OF THE WEIGHT-TRAINING PROGRAM

The structure of your weight-training program depends on your goals. Serious body builders may train 4 to 6 hours per day, 5 to 6 days per week, while "fitness addicts" incorporate weight training into programs involving other activities — such as aerobics, running, cycling, yoga, and swimming. Most people do not have that much time to devote to fitness training, and a commitment of a few hours a week will suit some people perfectly.

Number of Training Sessions per Week

Most people should train between 2 and 4 days per week. Two days per week is the minimum necessary to improve strength. After the early phases of training, 2 days per week tends only to maintain strength, rather than improve it. Training fewer than 2 days per week leads to muscle soreness and injury and is not recommended.

Excessive training often leads to overtraining and delayed progress. Studies show that heavy-training days invariably lead to tissue damage. Damaged tissue needs time to recover before the next intense session. Also, more training is not necessarily better training. Training intensity is the primary factor determining increased strength. A person who trains too often and too hard never recovers enough to train intensely. Sometimes it is better to rest than to train.

CAUTION ◆ Training too many days per week can lead to overtraining and injury. The body needs time to adapt. Sometimes, it is better to train less often but more intensely. Most experts recommend training 3 to 4 days per week.

Four-day-a-week programs are popular with some athletes trying to get into peak condition. Typically, they work the upper body 2 days per week and the lower body the other 2 days. For example, Monday and Thursday would be devoted to training the upper body, and Tuesday and Friday to the lower body. For most people, a 3-day-a-week schedule is optimal.

Warm-Up

Most experts agree that **warm-up** is essential before exercise, and empirical evidence suggests that warm-up improves performance and prevents injury. Warm-up raises body temperature so that the muscles respond better. It increases tissue blood flow and elasticity, making tissues less prone to injury. Warm-up also promotes joint lubrication. Intense exercise without warm-up may place the heart at risk.

CAUTION ◆ Always warm up before exercise. Adequate warm-up may enhance performance and prevent injury.

Warm-up can be either general or specific. General warm-up involves the whole body — large-muscle exercises such as jumping jacks, running in place, or stationary cycling.

Specific warm-up involves doing the same lift you intend to begin your program with, but using a lighter weight. For example, a person who plans to do 3 sets of 10 repetitions of 160-pound bench presses might do 1 set of 10 repetitions with 90 pounds as a warm-up. Do similar warm-up exercises for each major lift that forms your program.

Cool-Down

Cool-down returns muscle temperatures and metabolic rate to normal levels. Cool-down after weight training usually consists of relaxing. In contrast, after endurance exercise, it is important to gradually wind down the tempo of activity. Because weight training is not a continuous activity, winding down is unnecessary—unless you drastically increase your heart rate during the workout. In that case, do an active cool-down during recovery, such as riding a stationary bicycle at a slow cadence and no friction on the flywheel.

Many experts recommend stretching after a workout to help prevent muscle soreness. Also, this is a particularly good time to work on flexibility because the muscles and joints are warmed up.

Don't take a shower or whirlpool bath immediately after a vigorous weight-training workout. During intense training, blood shunts to the skin and muscles, and hormones mobilize to help you exercise. Taking a hot shower immediately after exercise places stress on the heart that some people may not be able to tolerate. Give yourself at least 5 to 10 minutes to relax first.

CAUTION	◆	Cool down after a workout before taking a hot shower or whirlpool bath. Exercise redirects blood to the skin for cooling and to the muscles for exercise metabolism. The combination of inadequate cool-down and exposure to a hot shower or whirlpool after exercise could result in fainting or other problems.

Choosing the Correct Weight

Don't use too much weight when you begin your program. For the first set, choose a weight that you can move easily for at least 10 repetitions. (Again, a repetition is one execution of the exercise, and a set is a group of repetitions followed by a rest.) If you aren't sure about a good starting weight, use only the barbell or the lowest weight on the exercise machine. You can always add weight later.

Do only one set of each exercise during the first workout. The exercises may feel very easy to do, but you must be careful not to overexert yourself. As discussed in Chapter 2, tissue damage causes muscle soreness 1 to 2 days after a workout. Some delayed-onset muscle soreness is very common, and perhaps necessary for improved strength, but excessive soreness suggests that you trained too hard.

Devote the first weeks of weight training to learning the exercises. Not only do you have to understand how to do the exercises, but your nervous system has to learn to communicate with the muscles so you can exert the necessary force. This takes time. Gradually add sets to your program. By the end of the second week of training, you should be doing a complete workout.

*later
10 rep = difficult*

During later training sessions, gradually add weight until you are bearing a significant load and the 10-repetition set becomes difficult. The time to add weight is when you can finish each set with relative ease. If you feel as though you can do 11 or 12 repetitions with a particular weight, it's time to add more resistance. If, after adding weight, you can do only 8 or 9 repetitions, stay with that weight until you can again complete the 10 repetitions per set. If, after adding weight, you can do only 4 to 6 repetitions, then you have added too much weight and must remove some.

Experienced weight trainers should avoid using too much weight after a layoff because they may get sore or injured. As described in Chapter 3, getting in shape gradually is a basic principle of training. Excessive training loads do not encourage the body to adapt faster; they only cause injury and delay progress.

| **CAUTION** | ◆ | Don't use too much weight after coming off a layoff from training because you may get sore or injured. |

Order of Exercises and Development of Antagonistic Muscle Groups

During weight training, smaller muscle groups fatigue more easily than larger ones. Therefore, do exercises that use more than one joint at a time (for example, bench presses, squats, or power cleans) before those using only one joint (for example, biceps curls, leg extensions, and wrist curls).

Most experienced weight trainers work one body part at a time. For example, they do all the leg exercises before doing upper-body exercises. Some even work lower-body and upper-body muscle groups on separate days. Intensity (i.e., the amount of weight used during the exercise) is the most important factor increasing strength. If you mix exercises for large- and small-muscle groups and those for the upper and lower parts of your body, you decrease the amount of weight you can use—and slow your progress.

Circuit training (performing a number of exercises rapidly in series) often purposely mixes exercises. This type of training is very effective for developing muscular endurance, but is less effective for gaining strength.

Include in your program exercises for antagonistic muscle groups. Muscles work a lot like a see-saw: Every movement initiated by a muscle group is opposed by an antagonistic muscle group. For example, the quadriceps muscles cause the knee to extend (straighten), while its antagonistic muscles, the hamstrings, cause it to flex (bend). If you develop the quadriceps muscles without working on the hamstrings, you create a muscular imbalance that can lead to injury and faulty movement patterns.

*Strength =
Fewer reps;
more weight*

Sets and Repetitions

Your goals determine the ideal number of **repetitions** and **sets.** Generally, if you want increased endurance, do more repetitions (10 or more) and more sets (3 or more). If increased strength is your primary goal, do fewer repetitions and use more weight.

Doing 4 to 6 repetitions per set for 1 to 5 sets is best for developing strength. People interested in doing single maximum lifts must occasionally do 1 to 3 repetition sets so they can adjust to the heavier weights. Experienced weight trainers use a variety of combinations

TABLE 5–3		
Example of a Beginning Weight-Training Program		
Exercise	*Sets*	*Repetitions*
Bench press	1–3	10
Lat pull	1–3	10
Lateral raise	1–3	10
Biceps curl	1–3	10
Triceps extension	1–3	10
Abdominal curl	1–3	10
Back hyperextension	1–3	10
Leg press	1–3	10
Calf raise	1–3	10

of sets and repetitions. (The next section, on cycling techniques, discusses some of these programs.)

Beginners should start off with more repetitions and lighter weights to give the tissues a chance to adjust to increased muscular loading and minimize the chances of injury. Start with 1 set of 8 to 10 repetitions of about 8 to 10 exercises. Practice this program, gradually increasing the weight, for at least 2 months, before decreasing repetitions in each set. If you want to progress more rapidly, try increasing the number of sets per exercise to 2 or 3. If rapid increases in strength are not too important to you, stay with 10 repetitions per set. An example of a beginning weight-training program appears in Table 5–3. You can do these exercises with free weights or weight machines.

Several training systems use a technique called **pyramiding,** which contains built-in warm-up. In pyramiding, practice an exercise for 3 or more sets, increasing the weight during each set. This technique was first introduced by T. L. DeLorme in the 1950s. DeLorme recommended 3 sets of 10 repetitions of each exercise. The resistance should progressively increase from 50 to 75 percent and 100 percent of maximum capacity.

There are many other systems for regulating loads, including the **constant set method, failure method, circuit training, super sets,** and **giant sets** (see Table 5–4 for examples of selected programs). Some of these techniques reduce the weight during later sets after reaching the maximum weight. Any technique you choose should allow you to warm up before significantly loading your muscles.

Basic Cycling Techniques

As mentioned in Chapter 3, many elite athletes use a powerful technique called cycle training, or periodization of training. This technique allows the body to adapt rapidly without overtraining and prepares it to accept and benefit from intense workouts.

In cycle training, the type, volume, and intensity of training are varied throughout the year. In athletics, the year is divided into off-season, preseason, early season, and peak season. The weight-training program is different during each part of the year.

TABLE 5–4
Selected Weight-Set-Repetition Methods

CIRCUIT TRAINING

Uses 6 to 20 exercise stations set up in a circuit (i.e., in series). The person progresses from one station to the next, either performing a given number of repetitions or doing as many repetitions as possible during a given time period (for example, 20 seconds) at each station.

CONSTANT SET METHOD

The same weight and number of sets and repetitions are used for each exercise. Example: Bench press 5 sets of 5 repetitions at 80 lb.

PYRAMID METHOD

Uses multiple progressive sets, either ascending or ascending–descending, for each exercise. Variations: increasing weight while decreasing repetitions or decreasing weight while increasing repetitions.

Ascending Pyramid

Set 1	5 repetitions	75 lb
Set 2	5 repetitions	100 lb
Set 3	5 repetitions	120 lb

Ascending–Descending Pyramid

Set 1	5 repetitions	75 lb
Set 2	5 repetitions	100 lb
Set 3	5 repetitions	120 lb
Set 4	5 repetitions	100 lb
Set 5	5 repetitions	75 lb

DeLORME METHOD

3 sets of 10 repetitions at 50, 75, and 100 percent of maximum. Example for a person who can do 10 repetitions at 100 lb:

Set 1	10 repetitions	50 lb (50%)
Set 2	10 repetitions	75 lb (75%)
Set 3	10 repetitions	100 lb (100%)

SUPER SETS

Usually uses two exercises, typically with opposing muscle groups, in rapid succession.

Set 1	10 repetitions	30 lb	knee extensions
Set 1	10 repetitions	15 lb	knee flexion
Rest			
Set 2	10 repetitions	30 lb	knee extensions
Set 2	10 repetitions	15 lb	knee flexion
Rest			
Repeat			

(Continued)

TABLE 5–4
Selected Weight-Set-Repetition Methods—*continued*

GIANT SETS

Uses multiple exercises in succession for the same muscle group.

Set 1	10 repetitions	75 lb	bench press
Set 1	10 repetitions	5 lb	dumbbell fly
Rest			
Set 1	10 repetitions	75 lb	bench press
Set 1	10 repetitions	5 lb	dumbbell fly
Rest			
Repeat			

During the off-season, athletes do general conditioning exercises. The program maintains fitness and provides mental and physical rest from the rigors of training. A tennis or field hockey player might run, play volleyball, swim, and do some circuit training. Light training in the sport maintains skill.

During the preseason and early season (sometimes called the load phase), if the goal is to develop maximum power for a strength–speed sport, such as track and field, the program develops base fitness—strength that serves as the basis for maximum lifts later in the season. The weight-training program involves much volume (5 sets of 5 to 8 repetitions for the major exercises, at moderately high intensities). This phase is typically very exhausting.

The peak phase (competitive phase) helps you achieve peak performance. The weight-training program involves high-intensity workouts with much less volume than in the pre- and early-season phases. The athlete gets plenty of rest between intense workouts, a technique that allows peak performance, or "peaking." If you time workouts and rest correctly, you can predict top performances.

Each major cycle contains microcycles in which the volume, intensity, and rest vary from workout to workout or from week to week. The purpose of microcycles is to allow muscle systems adequate recovery time. According to several studies, intensity is the chief factor in enhancing fitness. In traditional training programs, athletes train hard every session, which may lead to overtraining. Microcycles prepare people for intense training days by giving them time to recover.

In this way, cycle training encourages your body to adapt steadily with a minimum risk of injury. You make small, consistent gains over a long time. The system improves fitness, and peak performance happens at a predetermined time in the season. One basis for this method is that people adapt better to changing stimuli than to a constant program—partly because learning is fastest when a new activity is introduced and partly because change is psychologically stimulating.

Considerable muscle and connective tissue damage happen during and after intense endurance or strength training. Although scientists don't completely understand the relationship between tissue healing rate and the structure of the training program, common sense tells us there is such a relationship. Muscle fibers need to heal to some extent before you can safely stress them again.

TABLE 5–5
An Example of Cycle Training for General Conditioning

MONDAY

Exercise	Sets	Repetitions	Weight (lb)
Bench press	4	10	60
Lat pulls	3	10	30
Squats	4	10	80
Abdominal curls	3	20	—
Back extensions	3	15	—
Arm curls	3	10	25
Triceps extensions	3	10	15

WEDNESDAY

Exercise	Sets	Repetitions	Weight (lb)
Incline press	3	10	40
Modified pull-ups	5	5	—
Pull-overs	3	10	20
Leg presses	3	10	150 (machine)
Calf raises	4	20	150 (machine)
Abdominal curls	3	40	—
Good mornings	3	10	15

FRIDAY

Exercise	Sets	Repetitions	Weight (lb)
Bench press	3	10	50
Lat pulls	3	10	40
Squats	3	10	70
Abdominal curls	3	20	—
Back extensions	3	15	—
Arm curls	4	10	30
Triceps extensions	4	10	20

Note: Exercises can be done on weight machines or with free weights. Notice that exercises and the amount of weight used in an exercise vary from one workout to the next. Exercises are described in Chapters 6–11.

Cycle techniques are ideal for people doing general conditioning programs. It is unnecessary to do the same exercises every session using the same weights. Vary your program. Do some exercises intensely during one workout and other exercises intensely during the next. A basic 3-day-per-week conditioning program using the cycle-training technique appears in Table 5–5.

Making Progress

Initially, gains seem to come easily, but eventually you will reach a plateau where progress comes more slowly. Because the body adapts rapidly at first, many gains are due as much to learning new exercises as to actual changes in the muscles. The best thing to do when you're no longer improving is to examine your program. The cause is usually too much work, not enough work, or a bad program.

If you're working very hard every session and never miss a workout, and are still not making any progress, then maybe you're doing too much. Try cycling your workouts, or take a week or two off. Rest can do amazing things — often you can expect to return to personal records in the weight room if you just take a brief rest.

Sometimes you may not work hard enough. Are you only going through the motions when you train, not putting much effort into the exercises? Try adding more weight for at least one set of each exercise, even if it makes you do fewer repetitions. Make sure you complete each workout — cutting a few exercises out of the program each session can amount to a lot of work *not* accomplished after a few weeks.

Many people get enough rest and complete their workouts, but still don't make progress. You can often begin to make progress again by changing your program. Do exercises slightly different from the ones you usually do. For example, if you do bench presses on a machine or with barbells, try switching your program to include the press. Changing the way you do a lift sometimes helps you make progress. Having a spotter help you so you can use more weight may also help get you over the hump. If you are doing normal-grip bench presses, change your grip and do the exercise with a narrower or wider grip.

Another effective technique is to add exercises that strengthen muscles needed for the primary exercises. For example, doing bar dips is effective in improving the bench press. If you have trouble doing dips, have a spotter put his or her hands around your waist and help you with the movement. Knee extensions will improve the squat. Change the exercise, and your body will again adapt more quickly.

COMBINING WEIGHT TRAINING WITH OTHER SPORTS AND EXERCISES

Intense weight training is exhausting, thus interfering with performance in other activities. After a vigorous weight-training session, you may be more susceptible to injury if you immediately do another sport. If possible, get plenty of rest after an intense workout before doing a sport where you might get injured. If most of your program consists of general conditioning exercises, schedule strength and endurance workouts on different days. At least, schedule intense weight training on light endurance-training days. If you weight-train and have an aerobics class on the same day, go to the class first.

PREVENTING ACCIDENTS

Accidents and injuries do happen in weight training. Maximum physical effort, elaborate machinery, rapid movements, and heavy weights can combine to make the weight room a dangerous place if you don't take proper precautions. Table 5–6 presents the basic principles of preventing accidents in the weight room.

TABLE 5–6
Safety Rules for Weight Training

Weight training can be dangerous if safety guidelines are not followed. These are basic principles for preventing injuries in the weight room:
- Lift weights from a stabilized body position.
- Be aware of what is going on around you.
- Stay away from other people when they are doing exercises. Bumping into them could result in injury.
- Always use collars on barbells and dumbbells.
- Remain clear of the weight stack when someone else is using a weight machine.
- Don't use defective equipment. Report malfunctions immediately.
- Protect your back by maintaining control of your spine (protect your spine from dangerous positions). Observe proper lifting techniques, and use a weight-lifting belt for heavy lifts.
- Don't hold your breath. Avoid the Valsalva maneuver (trying to expire while holding your breath). This results in greatly reduced blood flow from the heart and could cause fainting.
- Always warm up before training.
- Don't exercise if you're ill.

Spotting

Spotters help the lifter during a failed repetition, help the lifter move the weight into position to begin a lift, actively help with the lift, and help during an unsuccessful repetition (Table 5–7). Helping with the weight after a failed repetition is the critical job of the spotter, who must be quick to go to the lifter's aid if necessary. You will need one or two spotters. During a bench press or an incline press, one spotter is sometimes preferable because it is easier to coordinate between one spotter and a lifter than between two spotters and a lifter. During a squat, you will need two spotters, one to stand on either side of the weight and help if the lift cannot be finished.

CAUTION ◆ Use spotters whenever you might be in danger of missing a lift and being caught under the fallen weight.

The lifter must indicate when he or she wants the weight removed. A spotter who removes the weight too soon may deprive the lifter of making a maximum effort and completing the lift. If there is too much delay in removing the weight, the lifter may get injured. Spotters must position themselves so as to be ready to help the lifter if needed, and they must use proper lifting techniques themselves: Bend the knees, maintain a straight back, and keep the weight close to the body (Figure 5–2). During the lift, spotters should be attentive but should not disrupt the lifter's concentration.

TABLE 5-7
Skills and Responsibilities of the Spotter

- Be strong enough to assist with the weight being lifted.
- Know the proper form of the exercise and the spot.
- Know the number of repetitions being attempted.
- Establish signals for beginning and ending the exercise with the lifter.
- Pay constant attention during the lift, but don't interfere unless necessary or requested.
- Pay particular attention to collars or weight plates that are sliding and if the weight trainer is using asymmetrical lifting techniques (i.e., moving one arm at a different speed than the other). These situations may require immediate intervention.

CAUTION   ◆   Spotters must be wary of injuring themselves. Use proper lifting techniques when spotting someone.

When you use spotters to help move a weight into position to begin an exercise, coordination between the spotters and you, the lifter, is important. Work out signals before the lift so that everyone understands when to raise the weight from the rack. For example, the lifter may count "one, two, three" with the weight being lifted into position on "three." It's best to work with the same spotters regularly because you'll learn what to expect from each other after a while.

Figure 5-2 Proper technique for spotting

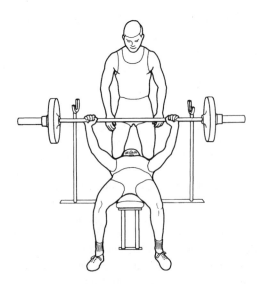

You will sometimes want a spotter to actively help with the exercise, using either free weights or weight machines. When doing negative exercises (eccentrics), the spotter may do most of the work for you during the active phase of the lift. The spotter can also provide just the extra amount of force needed to finish an exercise. Lifters sometimes call this help the "magic fingers" because the spotter may be able to help complete the lift by lifting with just a couple of fingers.

Collars

Collars secure weights to a barbell or dumbbell. Lifting weights without collars is dangerous. It is easy to lose your balance or to raise one side of the weight faster than the other. Without collars, the weights on one side of the bar will slip off, resulting in the weights on the opposite side crashing to the floor. Obviously this can knock you off balance and lead to injury. Clip collars, which weigh very little, are a good safety compromise for lifters who don't like to use standard collars.

| CAUTION | ◆ | Always use collars when lifting weights, and be sure they are secured properly. |

Preventing Accidents on Weight Machines

One of the attractions of weight machines is their safety. But weight machines are not totally harmless, so be cautious around them. Keep away from moving weight stacks. It's very easy for someone to jump on the machine ahead of you and begin an exercise while your fingers are close to the weight stack. Be particularly attentive when changing weights.

When doing exercises, don't be close to moving parts and weight plates. Also, don't walk near a machine when someone else is on it — you may break the person's concentration or collide with the moving machine.

Many weight machines can be adjusted to accommodate people of different sizes. Make sure the machine is properly adjusted and locked in place before beginning an exercise — it can be dangerous to begin an exercise only to have the machine move you suddenly.

Beware of broken machines. Broken bolts, frayed cables, broken chains, and loose cushions can give way and cause serious injury. If you notice a machine is broken or close to it, tell an instructor immediately.

Make sure the machines are clean. Equipment upholstery should be cleaned daily. Dirty vinyl is a breeding ground for germs that can cause skin diseases. A good practice is to carry a towel around with you and place it on the machine where you will sit or lie down. If you're sweating a lot, wipe down the upholstery with a towel after you finish the exercise.

Behavior in the Weight Room

Weight trainers should always have the utmost respect for the equipment because misuse can lead to a serious injury. Fooling around in the weight room can cause injury. Be attentive to what's happening around you.

Be courteous to others. When doing more than 1 set and other people are waiting to use the machine, let them do a set of the exercise while you are resting. Likewise, don't use exercise machines as resting stations. This disturbs other people's workout and slows the flow in the gym. Sign up for equipment that requires reservations — people tend to feel uncomfortable asking someone to get off a machine for which they have a reservation. Get off the machine when your time is up. The next person's workout is probably just as important to her or him as your workout is to you.

Medical Concerns

Report any obvious injury to muscles or joints to the instructor or a physician. Don't keep working out in the hope that the injury will go away. Training with an injured joint or muscle usually leads to more serious injury.

Be careful not to overdo. It's easy to strain or cramp a muscle by doing too many sets or repetitions. If you do injure yourself, either work on another body part or take the rest of the day off. Make sure you get the necessary first aid. Even minor injuries heal faster if you follow the "RICE" principle of treating injuries: Rest, Ice, Compression, Elevation.

Weight training tends to increase blood pressure, which in some people can cause serious medical problems. In people with coronary artery disease, weight training can cause symptoms such as arm or chest pain. Consult a physician if you are having any unusual symptoms during exercise or if you are not sure that weight training is a proper activity for you.

CAUTION   ◆   Report any headaches; chest, neck, or arm pains; dizziness; labored breathing; numbness; or visual disturbances to the instructor immediately.

PROPER MECHANICS OF EXERCISE

Each exercise has a proper technique. These techniques will be discussed in Chapters 6–11. Several principles, however, are common to all exercises. These principles will help you prevent injury and derive the maximum benefit from your weight-training program.

Lifting Techniques

Back injuries are among the most serious that can happen in the weight room. You can prevent them by following some basic principles of lifting:

- ◆ Keep the weight as close to your body as possible. The farther out you hold a weight from your body, the more strain on your back.
- ◆ Do most of your lifting with your legs. The large muscles of the thighs and buttocks are much stronger than those of the back, which are better suited to maintaining an erect posture. Keep your hips and buttocks tucked in.
- ◆ When picking up a weight from the ground, keep your back straight and your head level or up. Bending at your waist with straight legs places tremendous strain on the lower back muscles and spinal disks of the lower back.

- Don't twist your body while lifting. Twisting places an uneven load on back muscles, causing strain.
- Lift the weight smoothly, not with a jerking, rapid motion. Sudden motions place more stress on the spinal muscles and disks.
- Allow for adequate rest between lifts. Fatigue is a prime cause of back strain.
- Lift within your capacity. Don't lift beyond the limits of your strength.
- When training on a weight machine, make sure it is properly adjusted to your body. Uncomfortable, twisted positions may place unnecessary stress on vulnerable spinal muscles and nerves.

Breathing

Never hold your breath when lifting. Exhale when exerting the greatest force, and inhale when moving the weight into position for the active phase of the lift. Holding your breath while straining to perform a lift (called the Valsalva maneuver) causes a decrease in blood returning to the heart, which means that blood cannot be pumped as easily to the brain. It can cause dizziness and fainting.

Exercise Movements

Exercises should be done smoothly and in good form. With practice, you will "groove" your lift so that the weight is moved in the same general way every time you do the exercise.

Generally, move the weight into position for the active phase of the exercise slowly and with control. Lift or push the weight forcefully during the active phase of the lift. Obviously, if you are using enough resistance, these powered movements will be slow — but you should still try to do the movements explosively. An old weight-lifting saying to remember is to "go down slow and up fast."

Do not "bounce" the weight against your body during the exercise. Bouncing means that you make an explosive transition between the pushing and recovery phase of the lift. Advanced weight trainers sometimes do this so that they can practice an exercise using heavier weight. This practice is not recommended, however, because it can cause serious injury.

CAUTION   ◆   Never bounce a weight against the body.

Do all lifts through the full range of motion. Limiting the range of motion increases strength only in the part of the range you are exercising. Practiced correctly, weight training improves flexibility. "Muscle-boundness" — the inflexibility developed from weight training — happens only when exercises aren't done through a full range of motion.

Grips

Use the correct grip for each lift. There are three basic types of grip: **pronated** (palms away from you), **supinated** (palms toward you), and **dead-lift** grips (one palm toward you, one away). The pronated grip is used in most presses, pulls, and squats. The supinated grip is

Figure 5–3 Basic barbell grips: (a) pronated grip, (b) supinated grip, (c) dead-lift grip

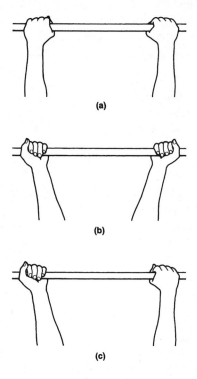

(a)

(b)

(c)

used in exercises such as biceps curls and chin-ups. The dead-lift grip is used in the dead-lift exercise to increase grip strength during the lift. (See Figure 5–3.)

The thumbless grip and thumblock grip are not recommended. The thumbless grip, as the name implies, involves placing the thumb in the same plane as the fingers. This grip, while placing the thumb under less stress, is dangerous. For example, in a bench press you could easily lose control of the weight, and it could fall on you. The thumblock grip, in which the thumb is wedged between the index and middle fingers, places the thumb at increased risk of injury.

6 Developing the Chest and Shoulders

CHEST AND SHOULDER EXERCISES ARE BY FAR THE MOST POPULAR WITH PEOPLE WHO TRAIN with weights. For women, these exercises improve the form of the chest and shoulders. For men, chest and shoulder exercises give them the T-shaped look of a powerful dynamo. Many sports require a strong upper body. Strong shoulder and chest muscles are an advantage when serving a tennis ball, for example, or rock climbing, or wind surfing. Chest and shoulder exercises build a strength and power that helps men and women excel in the activities they enjoy.

The chest and shoulders are more difficult to develop in women than men because women carry less muscle mass in that part of the body. Also, there is no exercise that will increase the size of women's breasts. Breast tissue is largely made of fat. If the size of the chest muscles is increased, the breasts may look a little larger. But because women have a limited ability to increase muscle size through weight training, the increase in breast size can be only minimal.

The major muscles of the chest and shoulders are **multipennate,** which means that the muscle fibers are aligned in several directions. Because of this, you should do several exercises to develop the muscles. For example, the pectoralis major muscle (the principal muscle of the chest) can be divided into upper, middle, and lower parts according to how the fibers are aligned. To completely train and develop this muscle, you must do exercises that build each of the muscle's three segments. Likewise, the deltoid (the principal muscle of the shoulder) is a three-part muscle that requires three or more exercises to develop fully.

It is extremely difficult to present exercises that functionally isolate specific muscle groups. For example, exercises for the chest, such as the bench press, also train the muscles of the arms, back, abdomen, and, to a limited extent, the legs (the legs stabilize the upper

59

body in some chest and shoulder exercises). Throughout Chapters 6–10, exercises are grouped according to the body part they work the best.

Also, it would be difficult and cumbersome to list exercises for every type of machine. Therefore, exercises that can be done using free weights and on Universal Gyms and Nautilus machines are presented. This is not an endorsement for these machines. Rather, exercises using them are presented because they are the most common machines found in schools and gyms in the United States and Canada and are popular with many recreational weight trainers. When using other machines, follow the basic guidelines for the machine exercises described in the text. They usually will be appropriate.

EXERCISES TO BUILD THE CHEST

The pectoralis major muscle is used in bringing the arm across the chest and lowering the arms when they are overhead. This muscle is very important in any movement that involves pushing. It is used during the forehand in tennis, when throwing a ball and blocking in football, and in freestyle swimming.

The principal exercises to develop the chest include:

- Bench press (barbell, dumbbell, power rack; chest press, Universal)
- Incline press (barbell, dumbbell; modified using incline bench and Universal shoulder press)
- Flys (dumbbell; 40-degree chest/shoulder, 10-degree chest, and arm-cross machines, Nautilus)
- Pullovers (barbell; pullover machine, Nautilus)
- Decline press (barbell, dumbbell; decline-press machine, Nautilus; modified chest press, Universal)
- Push-ups and modified push-ups

Bench Press

The bench press is probably the most popular weight-training exercise. Many people gauge strength by the amount of weight a person can "bench." Although the exercise is often overemphasized, it provides strength and power that can be carried over to many sports and develops well-shaped muscles that look good. This exercise primarily develops the chest, the front of the shoulders, and the back of the arms.

◆   THE TECHNIQUE   Lying on your back on a bench with your feet on the floor, grasp the bar at shoulder width with your palms upward, away from your body (Figure 6–1). Lower the bar to your chest, and then return it to the starting position. Try to push the bar straight up from the chest (nipple area in men and slightly below the breasts in women) to the starting position. Inhale when lowering the bar, and exhale when pushing it. Some people like to do this exercise with their feet on the bench because it helps prevent back arching. However, the legs are important stabilizers in this lift; you will be able to lift more weight if you place both feet on the floor.

Figure 6–1 (a, b) Bench press. (c) Narrow-grip bench press places more stress on the triceps muscles.

Muscles developed: pectoralis major, deltoid, triceps brachius

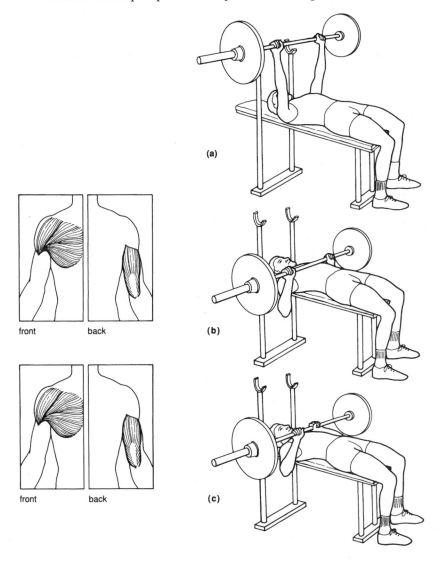

front   back   (a)

(b)

front   back   (c)

| CAUTION | ◆ | During the motion, be careful not to arch your neck or back because this could injure the spinal disks. Never bounce the weight off your chest because this could injure the ribs, sternum (breastbone), or internal organs. |

It is best to use a bench with a built-in rack constructed so that the weight can be taken on and off with little danger of pinching your hands. The rack and bench should be sturdy enough so that large weights can be supported safely. The bench should allow your arms and shoulders to travel freely during the exercise.

You can emphasize different muscle groups by varying the width of your grip. To increase the stress on the triceps muscle (muscle on back of your upper arms), narrow your grip; to stress the pectoralis muscle (chest), use a wider grip.

Chest Press, Universal Gym

◆   THE TECHNIQUE   Lying on your back on a bench with your feet on the floor and head toward the machine, grasp the handles at shoulder width with your palms upward (Figure 6–2). With the chest-press machine, the starting point of the exercise is with the handles at chest level. Push the handles upward until your arms are fully extended. Return to the starting position without banging the weights together. Exhale when pushing the weight, and inhale when lowering it.

Figure 6–2 Universal chest press
Muscles developed: pectoralis major, deltoid, triceps brachius

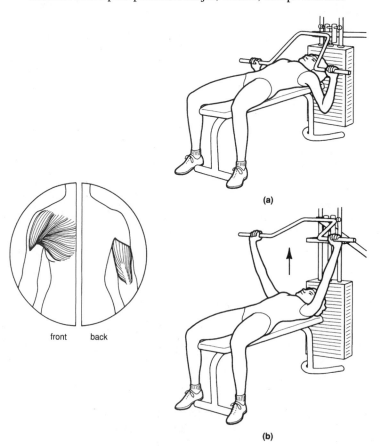

front   back

(a)

(b)

Universal recommends that you compensate for a stronger right or left arm by moving the hand of your weaker arm further out on the handle, about half again as far out as the other hand.

It is difficult to predict from performance on the Universal chest press how much weight you could lift with free weights. The chest press incorporates a device that progressively increases the resistance as you do the exercise. Thus, the weight is heavier at the end of the movement than at the beginning.

| **CAUTION** | ◆ | Be careful not to put your head too close to the weight stack when lying on the bench. Make sure the weight pin is fully inserted. |

Variations of the Bench Press

Variations of the bench-press lift will help increase your bench-press capacity or are good alternatives to it. These include the dumbbell bench press and power-rack bench press (Figures 6–3 and 6–4, respectively).

Dumbbell bench press   (Figure 6–3)

Figure 6–3 Dumbbell bench press
        Muscles developed: pectoralis major, deltoid, triceps brachius

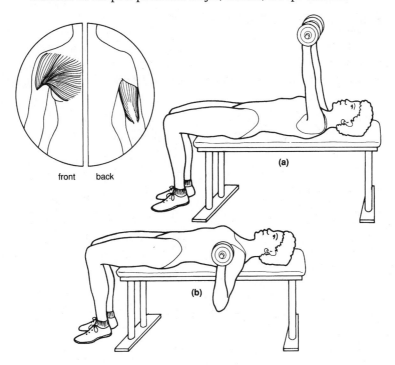

front   back

(a)

(b)

◆   **THE TECHNIQUE**   You will be able to handle only a fraction of the weight in the dumbbell bench press compared to the barbell bench press. To perform the dumbbell bench press, begin by sitting on the bench with dumbbells resting on your knees. Carefully rock backward until your back is on the bench and the dumbbells are in your hands and resting on your chest. Push the dumbbells overhead until your elbows are extended, then return the dumbbells to your chest.

Power-rack bench press   (Figure 6–4)

◆   THE TECHNIQUE   This exercise is used to help overcome sticking points you may experience during the bench press. The power rack allows you to place pegs, or stops, at various points within the vertical range of motion.

Place a bench inside of the power rack, and select three positions along the range of motion used during the exercise. The first pegs should be placed so the bar can rest close to your chest. Lying in the basic bench-press position with the bar resting on the first pegs, push the weight overhead. After you have completed your workout at the first pegs, move the pegs so that the bar rests in the middle of the range of motion. Repeat the exercise sequence. Finally, move the pegs so that the bar travels only a few inches during the exercise. At this level, you will be capable of handling much more weight than you can normally bench press. It's a safe way of getting used to increased weight.

Smith and Hammer machines   The Smith and Hammer Strength machines have become very popular in many gyms. Smith machines include an Olympic-type bar attached to a track. The bar has hooks on its ends to protect the person in the event the exercise can't be completed. Smith machines are particularly effective for doing bench presses, seated presses, and squats.

Hammer machines are a cross between free weights and traditional weight machines. Hammer press machines are very good for symmetrically developing the muscles on each side of the body because the machines are constructed so that each arm works indepen-

Figure 6–4 Power-rack bench press
Muscles developed: pectoralis major, deltoid, triceps brachius

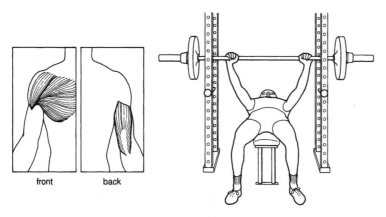

front   back

dently. Instructions for doing exercises on the Smith and Hammer Strength machines are similar to those for free weights and various other weight machines.

A number of auxiliary exercises can be included in the training program to help improve your bench press. Incline presses, flys, and parallel-bar dips are described in the following sections.

Incline Press

The incline press is similar to the bench press except that the path of the bar is at a 45-degree angle to the plane of the chest, rather than perpendicular to it. The exercise is performed while standing or sitting on a slant board. It develops the upper chest, the front of the shoulders, and the back of the arms, and tends to give the chest a rounder appearance. You can simulate the incline press on the Universal Gym by placing an incline bench within the shoulder-press machine.

◆   THE TECHNIQUE   Lying on an incline bench, grasp the bar at shoulder width and lower it to the upper part of your chest (Figure 6–5). Push the bar upward until your arms are extended. Remember that while pushing the weight, it is important to direct the bar upward toward the top of the head. Lower the weight to the starting position. Don't lower the bar farther down your chest. You will need spotters on this lift to handle maximal loads. A rack will also help you use heavier weight and will make spotting safer and easier.

CAUTION   ◆   Pushing the weight too far in front of you will make the exercise more difficult to perform and may result in a back, shoulder, or elbow injury.

Figure 6–5 Incline bench press
Muscles developed: upper pectoralis major, deltoid, triceps brachius

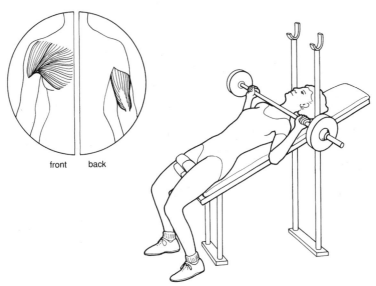

front   back

The incline press may be done with a barbell or with dumbbells. Special skill is required to lift dumbbells to the starting position of the exercise. While sitting or standing on the incline bench (depending on which type of bench you are using), grasp the dumbbells and place them on your knees. Beginning with the dumbbell in your left hand (if you are right-handed), vigorously flex your knee upward, pushing the dumbbell into the starting position. Repeat this procedure with your other arm. After completing the exercise, slowly lower the dumbbells, either one at a time or both together, back to the floor.

Modified Incline Press, Universal Gym

◆   THE TECHNIQUE   Place an incline bench (the long, straight type) between the handles of the shoulder-press station of the Universal Gym (Figure 6–6). You can also place blocks under a flat bench (a bench without racks) to simulate an incline bench. The bench should be aligned so that when you lie on it, your back is to the machine. Push the handles

Figure 6–6 Universal incline press
Muscles developed: upper pectoralis major, deltoid, triceps brachius

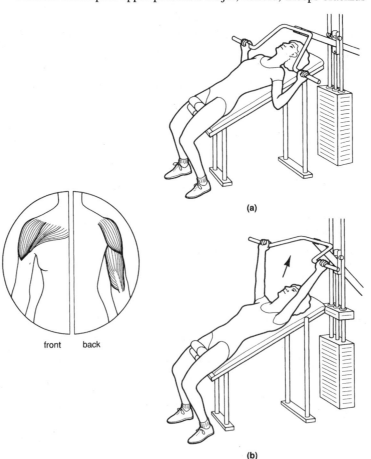

front   back

(a)

(b)

upward until your arms are extended, then lower the weight without banging the plates together.

Dumbbell Flys

Flys develop the chest and the front part of the shoulders (anterior deltoids). They are done with dumbbells or machines that simulate the use of dumbbells. Universal and Nautilus make machines that simulate this movement. This is a good exercise for developing the appearance of fullness of the chest.

◆   THE TECHNIQUE   Lie on a flat bench with a dumbbell in each hand, palms facing inward and arms extended straight above your chest. Keep your elbows bent slightly to prevent hyperextending them (Figure 6–7). Slowly lower the weights to the side until they reach shoulder level; then return to the starting position. As you get stronger, lower the weight below shoulder level. Do this exercise with arms straight or bent. Avoid straight-arm flys because of danger to the elbows. Flys can also be done on an incline or decline bench. Incline flys tend to work the upper part of the chest, whereas decline flys work the lower part of the chest.

| CAUTION | ◆   Don't use too much weight when you first start doing this exercise because there is a possibility of injuring your elbows. For the same reason, don't do straight-arm flys. |

Figure 6–7 Dumbbell flys: (a) bent arms, (b) straight arms
Muscles developed: pectoralis major, anterior deltoid

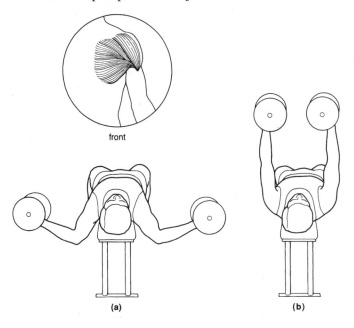

front

(a)   (b)

"Fly" Machines, Nautilus

Nautilus and several other equipment manufacturers make machines that simulate dumbbell flys. They may be superior to using free weights because they allow better isolation of the chest and shoulder muscles.

Arm cross ("pec deck")

◆   THE TECHNIQUE   The arm cross is part of the Nautilus double-chest machine (also includes decline press). Align the bench so that your upper arms are perpendicular to your torso (Figure 6–8). Sit back as far in the seat as you can so that you are exercising from a supported position. Grasp the handles so that your forearms are resting against the pads. You should feel a slight pull in your chest muscles in this starting position. Pushing with your forearms (not your hands), bring the elbows as close as you can in front of your chest. Universal, as well as several other manufacturers, make similar exercise machines.

Forty-degree chest/shoulder and ten-degree chest machines, Nautilus

◆   THE TECHNIQUE   These machines are similar in many ways to the arm-cross machine, except the incline benches are at different angles and they use large cylindrical pads rather than handles to move the weight (Figure 6–9). On each of these machines, adjust the

Figure 6–8 Nautilus arm cross
          Muscles developed: anterior deltoid, pectoralis major

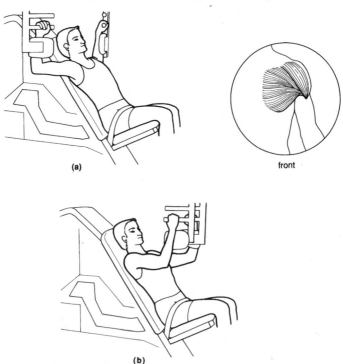

(a)

front

(b)

Figure 6–9 Nautilus 40-degree chest/shoulder, 10-degree chest machines
Muscles developed: pectoralis major, anterior deltoid

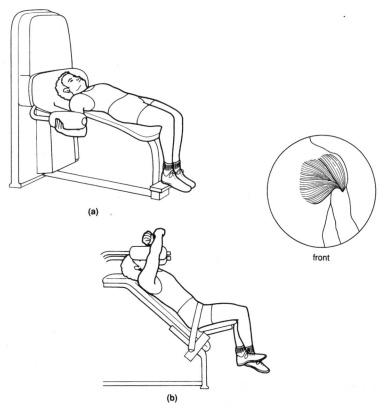

(a)

front

(b)

seat so that the tops of your shoulders are lined up with the cams of the machines (the movement points). Lying on the bench on your back, with your arms under the pads (pads should be placed at the bottom of your biceps muscles), move the pads together until they are over the center of your chest. Try to do the movement with your chest muscles as much as possible.

Pullovers

Pullovers are good for developing the pectoralis major, rib muscles, and lats (latissimus dorsi, a large muscle of the back). Pullovers can be done with either weights or machines.

◆   THE TECHNIQUE   Lie on your back on a bench; your head should be slightly above the end of the bench (Figure 6–10). Grasp a barbell with hands about 8 inches apart. With arms bent slightly, lower the bar behind your head and reach toward the floor. Return to the starting position. As a variation to bent-arm pullovers, you can work with straight arms, but then use less weight to prevent elbow injury.

You can also do these exercises on the low pulley station of the Universal Gym (Figure 6–11). The exercises are identical to those described for free weights, except they are done on the floor.

Figure 6-10 (a, b) Barbell bent-arm pullovers, (c, d) straight-arm pullover
Muscles developed: latissimus (back), pectoralis major (front)

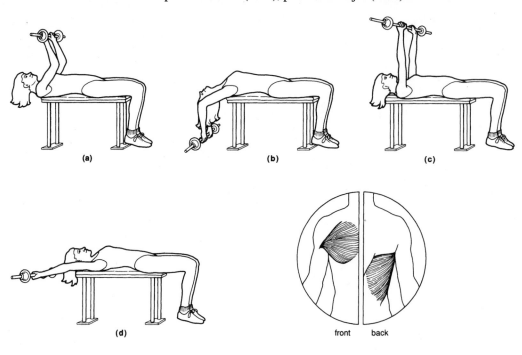

Figure 6-11 Universal Gym bent-arm pullovers
Muscles developed: latissimus dorsi, pectoralis major

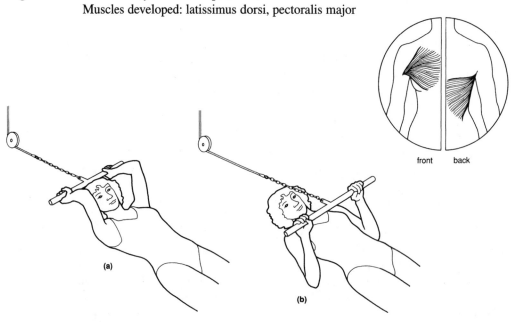

Figure 6–12 Dumbbell pullovers
              Muscles developed: pectoralis major (front), latissimus dorsi (back)

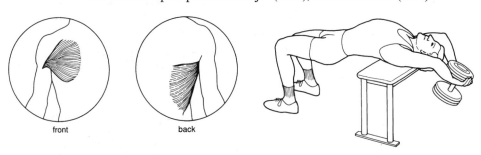

A single dumbbell can be used in place of the barbell. Generally, this exercise is accomplished with the bench placed perpendicular to the weight trainer (Figure 6–12).

Pullover Machine, Nautilus

◆   THE TECHNIQUE   Adjust the seat so that your shoulders are aligned with the cams (Figure 6–13). Push down on the foot pads with your feet so you can place your elbows on the pads. Rest your hands lightly on the bar. To get into the starting position, let your arms go backward as far as possible. Then pull your elbows forward until the bar almost touches your abdomen.

Figure 6–13 Nautilus pullover machine
              Muscles developed: pectoralis major (front), latissimus dorsi (back)

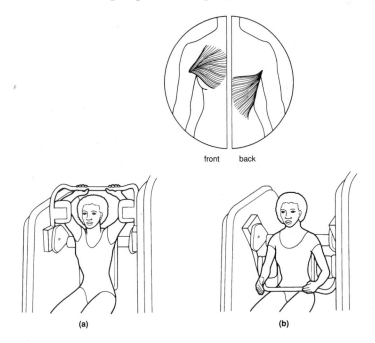

Decline-Bench Press

The decline press is not usually a part of the typical weight-training routine. Body builders use it to develop the lower part of the pectoralis major muscle. It also builds the front part of the shoulders and the backs of the arms.

Doing decline-bench presses with free weights requires a specialized piece of equipment called a "decline bench." A decline bench can be made by placing blocks under one end of a flat bench. Using this technique, you can do decline-bench presses on the Universal Gym. When using free weights, make sure the bench is steady and use spotters during the exercise. If you fail to complete this exercise, the weight could fall on your neck or face.

◆   THE TECHNIQUE   Lie on a decline bench, face up, with head downward (Figure 6–14). Grasp the weight at shoulder width, bring it to your chest, and then press it upward until elbows are extended. This exercise can also be done using dumbbells.

Decline Press, Nautilus Double-Chest Machine

A decline-press exercise station is part of the Nautilus double-chest machine.

◆   THE TECHNIQUE   Adjust the seat so that the tops of the handles are aligned at the tops of your armpits (Figure 6–15). Grasp the handles with palms toward you. Push the levers until your arms are fully extended.

Figure 6–14 Decline press
         Muscles developed: lower pectoralis major, deltoid, triceps

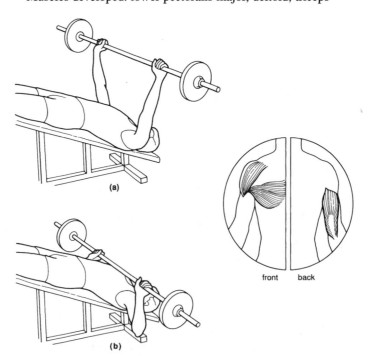

(a)

(b)

front   back

Figure 6–15 Nautilus decline press
Muscles developed: pectoralis major, deltoid, triceps

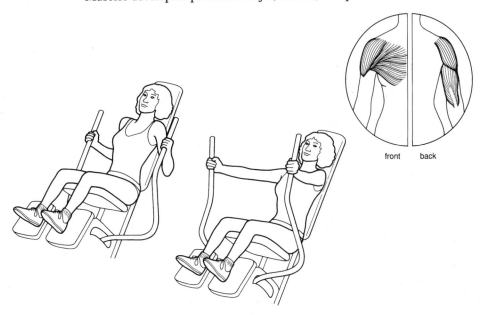

front   back

Push-Ups and Modified Push-Ups

Push-ups build the chest, shoulder, and arm muscles. Many people lack sufficient strength to perform even a single push-up when using standard push-up technique. The modified push-up, in which you support yourself with your knees, is less difficult than the standard technique. Use the modified technique if you can't do more than 8 standard push-ups. When you can do more than 30 modified push-ups, revert to the standard push-up technique.

◆   THE TECHNIQUE:

1. Starting position
    a. Standard push-ups: Start in the push-up position with your body supported by your hands and feet (Figure 6–16a).
    b. Modified push-ups: Start in the modified push-up position, with your body supported by your hands and knees (Figure 6–16b).

2. Lower your chest to the floor with your back straight, and then return to the starting position.

Figure 6–16 Push-ups

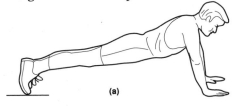

(a)

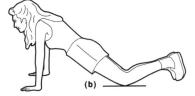

(b)

Other Exercises for the Chest

Many other exercises develop the chest muscles to some extent, including lat pulls, catching and throwing **medicine balls,** and "crushers" (specialized exercise devices that use movements resembling dumbbell flys). Horizontal push presses—in a standing position, push a weight horizontally as rapidly as possible—also develop the chest.

EXERCISES TO DEVELOP THE SHOULDERS

The shoulder is one of the most complex joints of the body, composed of six joints and more than twelve different muscles. The rest of this chapter focuses on the principal exercises that develop the shoulder's major muscle groups. Exercises to train the "rotator-cuff" muscles are also described. The rotator-cuff group, comprising four deep shoulder muscles, is important because it is often injured by swimmers and by baseball, volleyball, softball, and tennis players.

Although all the exercises described in the previous section ("Exercises to Build the Chest") train the shoulder muscles as well, the following exercises are generally recognized as the best for developing the major muscles of the shoulder:

- Overhead press (shoulder press)
- Behind-the-neck press
- Raises
- Upright rowing

Overhead Press

The overhead press, also known as the "military press," can be done standing or seated and with barbells or dumbbells. Universal and Nautilus, as well as many other manufacturers, make shoulder-press machines. This exercise develops the deltoids (the large triangular muscles covering the shoulder joints), upper chest, and the back of the arms. You should use a belt when doing unsupported overhead lifts, such as overhead presses.

CAUTION ◆   When standing, be careful not to arch your back excessively, or you may injure the spinal muscles, vertebrae (bones of the spine), or disks.

◆   THE TECHNIQUE   The overhead press with a barbell begins with the weight at your chest, preferably on racks. If you are a more advanced weight trainer, you can "clean" the weight to your chest, but attempt this only after instruction from a knowledgeable coach (Figure 6–17).

1. The clean: To perform the clean, place the bar on the floor in front of you. Keep your feet approximately 1 to 2 feet apart. Grasp the bar, palms

Figure 6–17 The power clean is often used to move the bar into the starting position for the overhead press.

Muscles developed: deltoid (front and back), triceps (back), trapezius (back)

down, with your hands at slightly more than shoulder width, and squat down, keeping your arms straight, your back at a 30-degree angle, and your head up. Pull the weight up past your knees to your chest while throwing your hips forward and shoulders back. Much of the power for the clean should come from your hips and legs.

Ask your weight-training instructor or coach to help you learn this lift because doing it improperly can lead to injury. If you are not an experienced weight trainer, use a rack to place the weights in the starting position.

CAUTION ◆ Do not attempt the clean unless you have some weight-training experience and receive proper instruction from a knowledgeable coach.

2. The overhead press: Push the weight overhead until your arms are extended, then return to the starting position (weight at chest). Again, be careful not to arch your back excessively.

Overhead-Press Machine, Nautilus

◆ THE TECHNIQUE Adjust the seat so the two bars are slightly above your shoulders (Figure 6–18). Sit down, facing away from the machine, and grasp the bars with palms facing inward. Press the weight upward until your arms are extended.

Figure 6–18 Nautilus overhead-press machine
Muscles developed: deltoid, triceps, trapezius

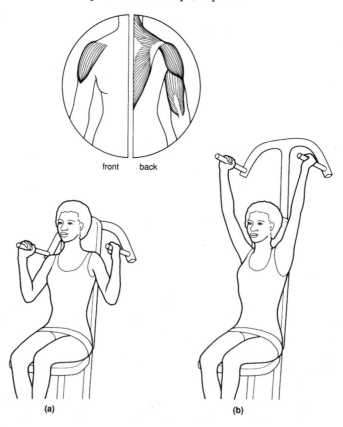

front   back

(a)   (b)

Overhead-Press Machine, Universal Gym

◆   THE TECHNIQUE   Place a high stool next to the overhead-press station so that when you sit down, either facing the machine or facing away from it, your shoulders almost touch the handles (Figure 6–19). Grasping the handles with hands facing the machine, push the bar overhead until your arms are extended. Don't arch your back or lean forward excessively. Try to do this exercise with your shoulders.

Behind-the-Neck Press

A variation of the standing press is the behind-the-neck press. This exercise develops the shoulders, back of the arms, and upper-back muscles. Avoid this exercise if you have a rotator-cuff injury because it can pinch sensitive tissues in the upper shoulder and make the condition worse.

◆   THE TECHNIQUE   This exercise can be done standing or seated and requires the use of a barbell. Use a rack to place the weight in the starting position (Figure 6–20). With a fairly wide grip, place the weight behind your head and rest it on your shoulders. Push the weight above your head until your elbows are extended and then return to the starting position.

Figure 6–19 Universal overhead-press machine
Muscles developed: deltoid, triceps, trapezius

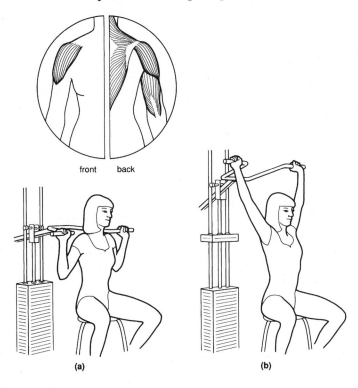

front   back

(a)   (b)

Figure 6–20 Behind-the-neck press—start; (b) behind-the-neck press—up
Muscles developed: deltoid, triceps, trapezius

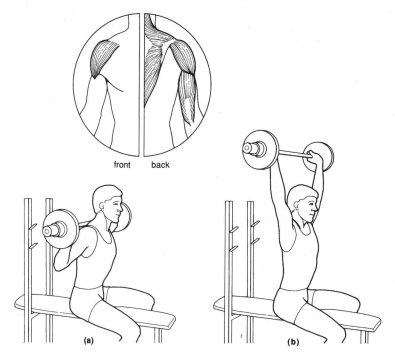

front   back

(a)   (b)

Behind-the-Neck Press, Universal Gym

◆   THE TECHNIQUE   This exercise is done exactly the same way as the seated press on the Universal Gym except that you face away from the machine instead of facing it. Start with the bar even or slightly in front of your shoulders to avoid strain on the rotator-cuff muscles.

Raises

Raises are used to develop the deltoid muscle, a three-part, round muscle making up the most prominent part of the shoulder. This exercise must be done to the front, side, and rear to develop the deltoid fully. Raises are usually done with dumbbells, although they can be done with wall pulleys or on specialized exercise machines (see Nautilus lateral-raise exercise below).

◆   THE TECHNIQUE   Lateral raises (Figure 6–21): From a standing position, with a dumbbell in each hand and arms straight, lift the weights on both sides until they reach shoulder level, then return to the starting position. Bend your arms slightly if your elbows hurt. Some people continue the exercise until the weights meet overhead, but this is inadvisable as it may injure the shoulders. Lateral raises develop the middle section of the deltoid muscle.

◆   THE TECHNIQUE   Front raises (Figure 6–22): In a standing position, using dumbbells or a barbell, and with arms straight, lift the bar in front of you to shoulder level, then return to starting position. This exercise develops the front part of the deltoid muscle.

Figure 6–21 Lateral raises
Muscles developed: middle deltoid

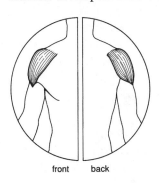

front   back

Figure 6–22 Front raises
Muscles developed: anterior deltoid

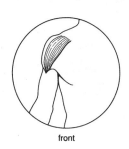

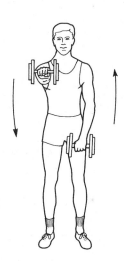

front

Figure 6–23 Bent-over lateral raises
Muscles developed: posterior deltoid, trapezius

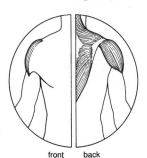

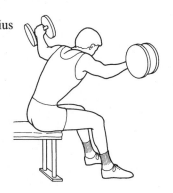

front   back

◆   THE TECHNIQUE   Rear (bent-over) lateral raises (Figure 6–23): This exercise requires dumbbells. In a standing or seated position, with knees bent slightly, bend at the waist. Lift the weights to the side until they reach shoulder level; return to the starting position. Bent-over lateral raises develop the back portion of the deltoids.

Lateral-Raise Machine, Nautilus

◆   THE TECHNIQUE   Adjust the seat so that pads rest just above your elbows when your arms are at your sides and your hands are forward (Figure 6–24). Lightly grasp the handles and push the pads to shoulder level with your arms. Return to the starting position. Lead the movement with your elbows rather than trying to lift the bars with your hands.

Seventy-Degree Shoulder Machine, Nautilus

◆   THE TECHNIQUE   Set the seat so that the cams are even with your shoulders (Figure 6–25). Place your arms under the pads so that they rest just below your biceps muscles on the inside of the elbow joint. Move both arms toward the middle of your chest until the two pads almost touch. Return to the starting position.

Upright Rowing

Upright rowing develops the shoulders, the front of the arms, the neck, and the upper back. Because it affects so many large-muscle groups at the same time, it is an excellent upper-body exercise.

Figure 6–24 Nautilus lateral-raise machine
Muscles developed: deltoid

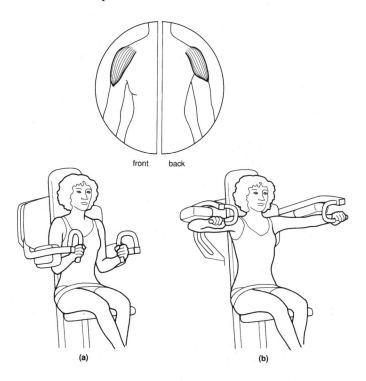

front   back

(a)   (b)

Figure 6–25 Nautilus 70-degree shoulder machine
Muscles developed: deltoid, pectoralis major

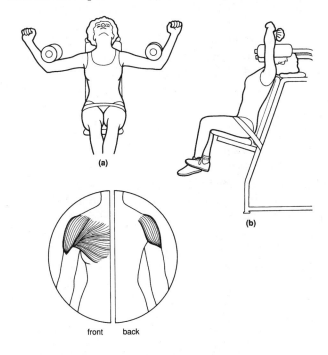

Figure 6–26 Upright rowing
Muscles developed: deltoid (front), trapezius (back), rhomboid (back)

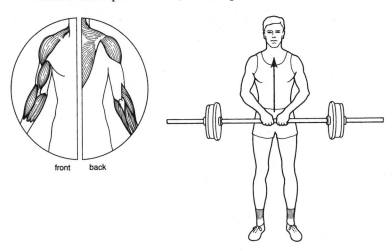

◆   THE TECHNIQUE   Using a pronated grip, grasp a barbell with hands close together and stand with the weight at waist level (Figure 6–26). Pull the weight to the upper part of your chest, then return to the starting position.

Upright Rowing, Universal Gym

◆   THE TECHNIQUE   Upright rowing on the Universal Gym uses the same basic technique as with free weights. Adjust the chain of the low pulley station so that the weights you're using go above the weight stack when you stand with the bar at your abdomen (Figure 6–27). With hands at waist level, grasp the bar with palms away from you (pronated grip) (starting position). Stand far enough away so that the cable does not touch the weight stack.

Rotator-Cuff Exercises

The rotator cuff of the shoulder is composed of four muscles that cause the humerus (the large bone of the upper arm) to rotate (turn) inward and outward. This muscle group is often injured in activities that require the arm to go above shoulder level, such as swimming, tennis, and throwing. The best way to prevent injuries is to make the muscles strong and flexible. Three exercises to strengthen this muscle group include:

◆ Dumbbell external rotation
◆ Dumbbell internal rotation
◆ Empty-can exercise

Dumbbell External Rotation

This exercise strengthens muscles that cause the arm to rotate outward (infraspinatus and teres minor).

Figure 6–27 Universal upright-rowing machine
Muscles developed: deltoid, trapezius, rhomboid

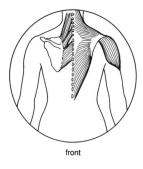

front

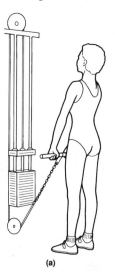

(a)

(b)

Figure 6–28 Exercise to strengthen shoulder external rotator muscles
Muscles developed: infraspinatus, teres minor

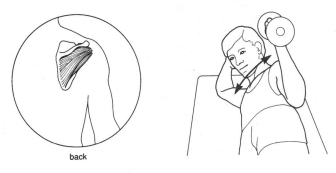

back

Figure 6–29 Exercise to strengthen shoulder internal rotator muscles
Muscles developed: subscapularis

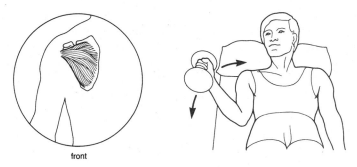

front

◆   THE TECHNIQUE   Lie on your side on a table, resting on one elbow (Figure 6–28). Bend your other elbow halfway (90 degrees), keeping the elbow tight to the rib cage. Slowly lower the weight, and then lift it back to the starting position.

Dumbbell Internal Rotation

This exercise develops the muscles that cause the shoulder to rotate inward (subscapularis).

◆   THE TECHNIQUE   Lie on your back on a table with your elbow bent halfway (90 degrees) and held tightly against your side and with your hand extended over your chest (Figure 6–29). Slowly lower the weight to your side, and then slowly lift it back to the starting position.

Empty-Can Exercise

This is probably the most important rotator-cuff exercise because it strengthens the supraspinatus muscle, the muscle of the rotator-cuff group that is most often injured in sports.

Figure 6–30 Empty-can exercise to strengthen the supraspinatus
Muscles developed: supraspinatus, deltoid

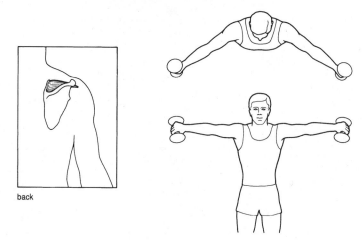

back

◆   THE TECHNIQUE   Stand upright and hold a dumbbell in each hand (Figure 6–30).
Keeping your arms straight, raise your arms to shoulder height, move them horizontally
about 30 degrees, and rotate them inwardly as much as possible so that the palms are facing the floor. Slowly lower and raise the weights through a 45-degree arc. It looks as if you
are emptying liquid from two cans—that's how the exercise got its name.

7 Developing the Arms

WE USE OUR ARMS FOR ALMOST EVERY ACTIVITY IN WORK AND PLAY. IT HELPS TO HAVE strong arms for a wide variety of tasks — gardening, opening jars, throwing a ball, or playing tennis. Strong, attractive arms are within reach of anyone who will devote a little time to developing them. This chapter presents basic arm and forearm exercises as well as specializing arm exercises for preventing "tennis elbow" and increasing grip strength. For the sake of this discussion, exercises for the arm will be divided into three categories: the front of the arm, the back of the arm, and the forearm.

EXERCISES FOR THE FRONT OF THE ARM

Curls are the best exercises for developing the muscles of the front of the arm. The principal muscles of this area include the biceps brachius and the brachialis. Curls can be done using a barbell, dumbbells, special curl bars, or curl machines. Curl bars (Figure 7–1) are useful because they reduce stress on the forearm muscles. They allow you to use more weight and prevent injury to your forearms. Among the many variations of curl exercises are the following:

◆ Standing barbell curls
◆ Dumbbell curls

Figure 7–1 The curl bar

- Preacher curls
- Reverse curls
- Curl machine, Nautilus
- Double-arm curls, low pulley station, Universal Gym

Standing Barbell Curls

This is the old standby for developing biceps strength. Be sure not to bend your back when doing this exercise or you may hurt yourself. If you use heavy weights, it's a good idea to use a weight-lifting belt. If your forearms get sore after a few weeks, you probably are straining the muscles. Switch from a straight bar to a curl bar.

◆   THE TECHNIQUE   From a standing position, grasp the bar with your palms upward, your hands shoulder-width apart (Figure 7–2). Keeping your upper body rigid, bend (flex) your elbows until the bar reaches a level slightly below the collarbone. Return the bar to the starting position.

CAUTION   ◆   To avoid injury, do not arch your back during this exercise. Standing with your back against the wall will help keep your back straight. If you are lifting heavy weights, use a weight-lifting belt.

Figure 7–2 Standing barbell curl
Muscles developed: biceps, brachialis

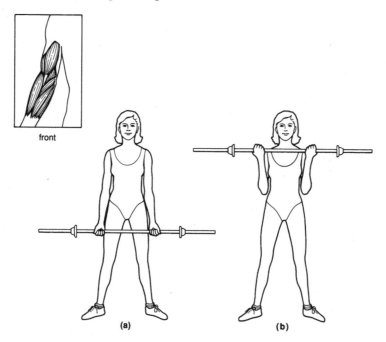

front

(a)   (b)

Dumbbell Curls

There are many ways of doing dumbbell curls—seated on a flat bench or seated on an incline bench; alternating between arms, doing both arms at the same time, and doing all the repetitions with one arm before doing them for the other arm. Although there is little difference between these lifts, each lift stresses the arm in a slightly different way. You can change your routine with these variations to add interest to your program.

◆   THE TECHNIQUE   While seated on a flat or incline bench, grasp the dumbbells using a supine grip (palms up) (Figure 7–3). Begin with the arms extended, bend the arms until the weights approach your shoulders, and then return to the starting position. Swinging the weights or bending your back while doing dumbbell curls will make the exercise less effective.

Preacher Curls

Preacher curls effectively isolate the biceps, the muscles of the front of the arm. This lift is so effective because it is extremely difficult to cheat while doing it. It requires a special apparatus called a "preacher stand," so named because it resembles a pulpit. If a preacher stand is not available, an incline bench can be substituted.

◆   THE TECHNIQUE   This lift can be done using a barbell, dumbbells, or curl bar. Using a supinated grip, place your elbows on the preacher stand and fully extend your elbows. Bend your arms ("curl" the weight) until they almost reach your collarbone; then return to the starting position (Figure 7–4). With dumbbells, this exercise can be done one arm at a time.

Figure 7–3 Seated dumbbell curl
          Muscles developed: biceps, brachialis

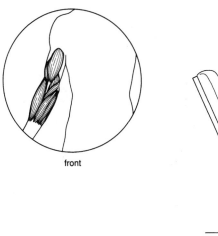

front

Figure 7–4 Preacher curls using preacher stand
Muscles developed: biceps, brachialis

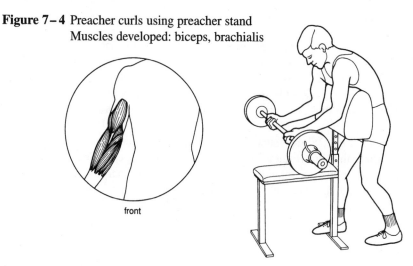

front

Reverse Curls

Reverse curls have an effect similar to that of preacher curls, except they place a different stress on the forearm muscles. You can do this exercise with a barbell, dumbbell, or curl bar, and in a seated or standing position.

◆   THE TECHNIQUE   Stand holding the weight at your waist, using a pronated grip (palms down, opposite of preacher curls). Lift the weight by bending at your elbows until the bar almost reaches your collarbone; then return to the starting position (Figure 7–5).

Figure 7–5 Reverse curls (note grip)
Muscles developed: biceps, brachialis, brachioradialis

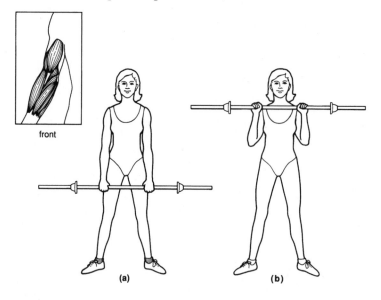

front

(a)   (b)

Curl Machine (Multibiceps), Nautilus

This machine resembles the preacher-curl exercise with free weights. It is excellent for isolating the biceps muscle.

◆   THE TECHNIQUE   Adjust the seat so that your upper arms are almost parallel to the supporting pad (Figure 7–6). You should be able to comfortably bend your arms through their full range of motion. Grasp the handles and extend your lower arms (starting position). Flex your arms as much as possible while keeping your elbows on the supporting pad; then return to the starting position.

Double-Arm Curls, Low Pulley Station, Universal Gym

The same basic technique is used for curls on the Universal Gym as with free weights.

◆   THE TECHNIQUE   Adjust the chain of the low pulley station so that the weights you're using go above the weight stack when you stand with the bar at your abdomen (Figure 7–7). With hands at waist level, grasp the bar with a supinated grip (starting position). Keeping your elbows close to your sides, curl your elbows until the weight touches your upper chest; then return to the starting position.

Figure 7–6 Nautilus curl (multibiceps) machine
Muscles developed: biceps, brachialis

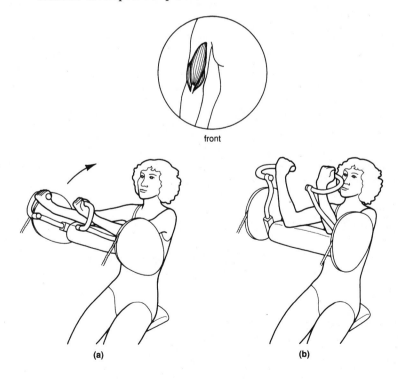

front

(a)   (b)

Figure 7–7 Double-arm curls, low pulley station, Universal Gym
Muscles developed: biceps, brachialis

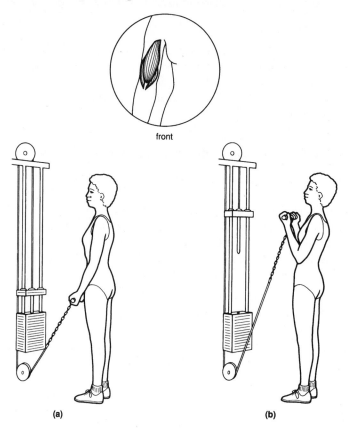

Other Exercises for the Front of the Arm

Any exercise that adds stress to the arm muscles as you bend your elbow will work this part of your body. Exercises that work the biceps, as well as other muscles, include pull-ups, chin-ups, lat pulls, and rowing exercises.

EXERCISES FOR THE BACK OF THE ARM

The triceps is the major muscle of the back of the arm and is trained during all pressing exercises. Examples of exercises that are particularly good for building the triceps include the following:

- ◆ Triceps extensions on the lat machine
- ◆ French curls
- ◆ Bench triceps extensions

Figure 7–8 Triceps extension on the lat machine
Muscles developed: triceps

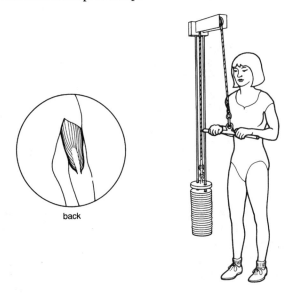

back

♦   Parallel-bar dips

♦   Chair dips

♦   Triceps extensions, Nautilus multitriceps machine

Triceps Extensions on the Lat Machine

The triceps extension on the lat machine is an excellent exercise for isolating the triceps muscles. This exercise can be done on the Universal Gym, or Nautilus lat-machine stations, or on a freestanding lat machine. If you develop elbow pain as a result of doing this exercise, try another of the triceps exercises listed previously.

♦   THE TECHNIQUE   Using a narrow, pronated grip, grasp the bar of the lat machine and fully extend your arms with your elbows held closely at your side (Figure 7–8). From this starting position, with elbows locked to your side, allow your hands to be pulled up to your chest; then firmly push the weight back to the starting position. If your elbows move during this exercise, you are cheating.

French Curls

This exercise appears to be similar to the behind-the-neck press, which develops the shoulders (see Chapter 6), but done properly it is very effective in isolating the triceps. The basic difference between the two exercises is that the behind-the-neck press involves movement of both the shoulder and elbow joints, whereas in French curls the shoulders are fixed and the movement occurs in the elbows.

Figure 7–9 French curls (seated triceps extensions)
Muscles developed: triceps

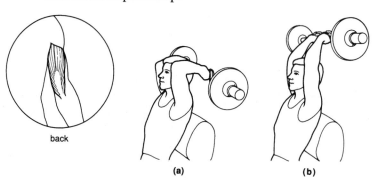

(a)   (b)

◆   THE TECHNIQUE   Grasp a barbell behind your head, using a pronated grip with your hands approximately 6 to 12 inches apart (Figure 7–9). Keeping your elbows up and stationary, extend your arms until the weight is overhead; then return to the starting position. Although somewhat awkward, this exercise can also be done using one handle on the seated press station of the Universal Gym.

Bench Triceps Extensions

This exercise is similar in many ways to French curls.

CAUTION ◆   Be careful not to use too much weight; if you lose control of the bar during the exercise, you could seriously injure yourself.

◆   THE TECHNIQUE   Lie on a bench, grasping a barbell with a pronated grip, hands 6 to 12 inches apart (Figure 7–10). Push the weight above your chest until your arms are extended (starting position). Keeping your elbows in a fixed position, carefully lower the weight until it touches your forehead, and then push the weight back to the starting position.

Figure 7–10 Bench triceps extension
Muscles developed: triceps

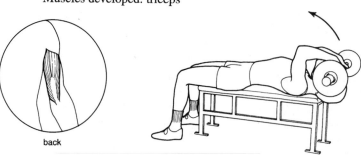

Parallel-Bar Dips

This exercise is excellent for helping you improve your bench press as well as building your triceps. Several equipment manufacturers make parallel-bar-dip machines that actively assist you with the movement.

◆   THE TECHNIQUE   Support yourself between the parallel bars on your fully extended elbows (Figure 7–11). Lower yourself by slowly bending your elbows until your chest is almost even with the bars. Then push up until you reach the starting position. A good way to improve if you can't do any repetitions initially is to have someone hold your waist and assist you during the motion.

Chair Dips

This exercise is similar to parallel-bar dips, and you can do it at home using a couple of chairs.

◆   THE TECHNIQUE   Support yourself between two sturdy chairs placed slightly more than shoulder width apart (Figure 7–12). Face toward the ceiling with your elbows and legs fully extended. Lower yourself by slowly bending your elbows. Then push up until you reach the starting position.

Triceps Extensions, Nautilus Multitriceps Machine

The Nautilus multitriceps machine is excellent for isolating the triceps muscle.

◆   THE TECHNIQUE   Adjust the seat so that when you sit down, your elbows are slightly lower than your shoulders (Figure 7–13). Place your elbows on the support cushion and your forearms on bar pads (starting position). Extend your elbows as much as possible; then return to the starting position.

Figure 7–11 Parallel-bar dips
Muscles developed: triceps, trapezius, deltoid, latissimus dorsi, pectoralis major

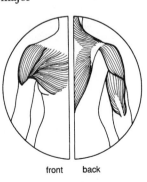

front   back

Figure 7–12 Chair dips
Muscles developed: triceps, trapezius, deltoid, latissimus dorsi, pectoralis major

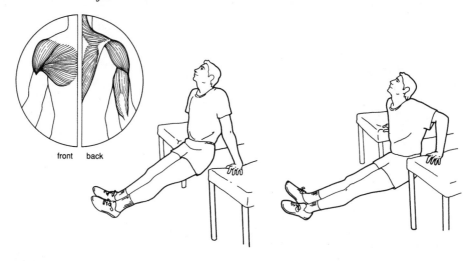

Figure 7–13 Nautilus multitriceps machine
Muscles developed: triceps

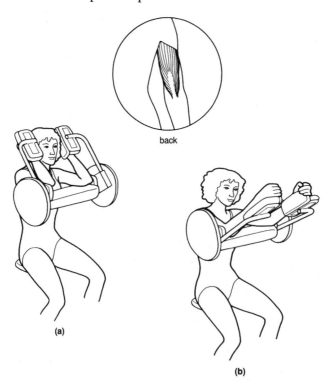

EXERCISES FOR THE FOREARM

The forearm muscles are essential to any activity requiring a rapid wrist movement (snap), such as in golf, the tennis serve, badminton, and throwing a ball. Weakness or overuse of the forearm muscles results in tennis or carpenter's elbow. The forearm muscles are also largely responsible for grip strength. Exercises that develop the forearm muscles include the following:

- ◆ Wrist curls
- ◆ Wrist rollers
- ◆ Wrist rollers, Universal Gym

Wrist Curls

Wrist curls are done using either a supinated or pronated grip. Supinated wrist curls build the forearm flexors and are important accessory exercises to biceps curls. Pronated or reverse wrist curls build the wrist extensors, the muscles injured in tennis elbow.

◆ THE TECHNIQUE   You can do this exercise with either a barbell or dumbbells. In a seated position, with forearms resting on your thighs and hands extending over your knees, using a supinated grip, lower the weight as far as possible; then lift your hands upward ("curl" your wrists) by bending at the wrists as much as you can (Figure 7–14). Repeat this exercise using a pronated grip. You can do wrist curls on the Universal Gym using the low pulley station with either the handles or small bar.

A variation of this exercise is the lateral wrist curl. It requires the use of a small bar with the weight affixed at one end. Do the exercise in the same manner as for wrist curls, except bend your wrist to the side.

Wrist Rollers

This exercise requires a machine, such as the wrist-roller station on the Universal Gym, or a wrist-roller device. The device can be purchased or constructed. To make one, drill a hole through a cylindrical piece of wood and tie a 3-foot piece of rope or small chain to it. Then attach the weight to the other end of the rope.

◆ THE TECHNIQUE   While holding the piece of wood out in front of you with both hands and using a pronated grip, lift the weight by winding the rope around the wood (Figure 7–15).

Wrist Rollers, Universal Gym

The wrist-roller station on the Universal Gym is much easier to use than the wrist-roller device. You can do wrist curls (wrist rollers), reverse wrist curls (reverse wrist rollers), forearm supination (turn palms up), forearm pronation (turn palms down), and lateral wrist curls.

Figure 7–14 Wrist curls (a) extension, (b) flexion, and (c) using two dumbbells at once
Muscles developed, wrist extension (a): extensor carpi radialis longus, extensor carpi radialis brevis, extensor carpi ulnaris
Muscles developed, wrist flexion (b): flexor carpi radialis, flexor carpi ulnaris

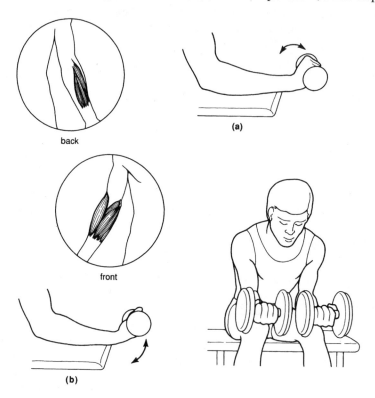

back

front

(a)

(b)

Figure 7–15 Wrist rollers
Muscles developed: flexor carpi radialis, flexor carpi ulnaris

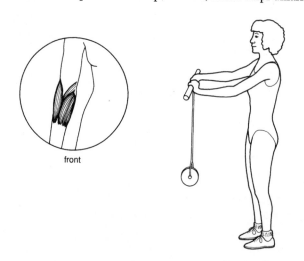

front

Figure 7–16 Wrist curls on the Universal Gym
Muscles developed, wrist extensions (a, b): extensor carpi radialis longus, extensor carpi radialis brevis, extensor carpi ulnaris
Muscles developed, wrist flexion (c, d): flexor carpi radialis, flexor carpi ulnaris

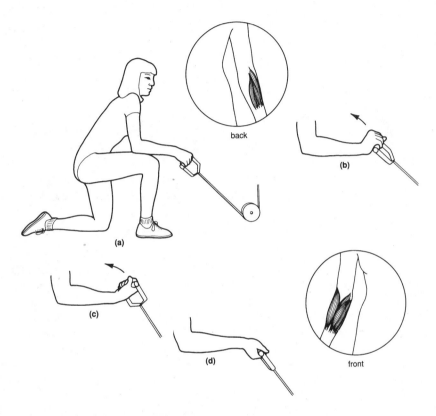

◆   THE TECHNIQUE   To do wrist rollers on the Universal Gym, place both hands on the grips and turn the handles clockwise (forward) (Figure 7–16). When your palms are facing up, this exercise builds the muscles on the front of your forearms. Reverse wrist rollers are the same, except you turn the handles counterclockwise.

Other Exercises for the Forearm and Grip

Grip strength is very important in certain sports—tennis, softball, and rock climbing, for example. People often don't have very good grips because they don't work to develop them. Serious weight-trained athletes have very strong forearms and grips. Yet few of them do wrist rollers or wrist curls. Large-muscle weight lifts, such as cleans, snatches, and dead lifts, place considerable stress on the forearms and hands. If you do those kinds of lifts, you will develop a good grip and strong forearms—especially if you do these lifts without lifting straps.

If you don't want to do these exercises, carry around a small rubber ball and squeeze it every time it occurs to you. This isometric exercise is very effective for developing grip and forearm strength.

8 Developing the Neck and Back

MOST PEOPLE HAVE TROUBLE WITH THEIR NECK AND BACK AT SOME POINT DURING THEIR lifetime, yet this part of the body is often neglected by weight trainers.

The spine is composed of a series of bones called vertebrae, with the spinal cord running through a channel in these bones. In between each vertebra lie shock absorbers, the "intervertebral disks." The vertebrae have three natural curves, which aid the disks in absorbing shock. Strong muscles are important for maintaining these curves.

Weight trainers must take special care to select exercises that do not damage the intervertebral disks. Nerves that emerge from the spinal cord act as messengers between the tissues and the central nervous system. Pain and muscle spasm result if abnormal pressure is put on these nerves. Strong neck and back muscles help maintain the proper alignment in the vertebrae and prevent pressure on the spinal nerves.

Strong neck and back muscles are critical for movement. Because the neck controls the movement of the head, strong neck muscles are important in any sport. The middle- and upper-back muscles are also vital in almost all movements and provide a balance to the muscles of the front of the body. The lower-back muscles help maintain the body in an upright posture and are important in bending movements. Because the low back is notoriously vulnerable to injury, these muscles must be kept strong and flexible.

The following exercises are divided into three parts—exercises for the neck, the upper back, and the lower back. Considerable overlap exists among these areas, and exercises described in other parts of the book often affect the neck and back.

EXERCISES FOR THE NECK

Strong neck muscles are important for all active people. Most people do not follow a systematic program for strengthening the neck muscles, even though the neck is vulnerable to serious injury. Neck pain affects many people, often because of poor strength in the neck and upper-back muscles. Including basic neck-strengthening exercises in the weight-training program could help prevent neck injuries.

The intensity of neck exercise should be increased gradually, particularly if you are recovering from a neck injury or have neck pain. Neck muscles are relatively small and thus more susceptible than larger muscles to the destructive effects of sudden overload.

Four basic techniques for strengthening the neck are:

- Manual-resistance exercises
- Isometric neck exercises
- Neck-harness exercises
- Neck-machine exercises

Manual-Resistance Exercises

Manual-resistance neck exercises provide an exercise load in all neck motions. These exercises are an easy, inexpensive way to strengthen neck muscles and can be incorporated almost anywhere in the program. For example, they can be added to your stretching routine prior to running or included as one of your weight-training exercises.

| CAUTION | ◆ Extreme care is essential: Manual resistance can be very dangerous if you use excessive force. Have your physical therapist, doctor, or coach instruct you in proper technique before attempting these exercises. |

Do these exercises on only one side of the body at a time. Do not cross the body's midline. Three movements should be used in your manual-resistance neck-training program: flexion, extension, and lateral flexion. Neck flexion is when you bring your chin toward your chest; neck extension is when you tilt from a flexed to neutral position; and neck lateral flexion is when you tilt your head to the side. Do not hyperextend the neck (i.e., extend the head backward past the midline of the body) because this could cause injury.

◆   THE TECHNIQUE   Manual neck flexion (Figure 8–1): Lie on your back on a bench or table, with your head hanging over the edge. Have your training partner supply resistance

Figure 8–1 Manual neck flexion
Muscles developed: sternocleidomastoideus, scaleni

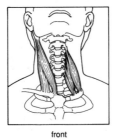

front

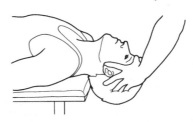

to your forehead as you attempt to bring your chin to your chest. Apply minimal resistance when you first start doing this exercise.

◆   THE TECHNIQUE   Manual neck extension (Figure 8–2): Lie on your stomach on a bench or table with your head hanging over the edge. Have your training partner supply resistance to the back of your head as you attempt to bring it toward the back of your spine. Again, extend your head only to the midline of your body.

◆   THE TECHNIQUE   Manual neck lateral flexion (Figure 8–3): Lie on your side on a bench or table with your head hanging over the edge. Have your training partner sup-

Figure 8–2 Manual neck extension
   Muscles developed: splenius capitus, splenius cervicus, trapezius

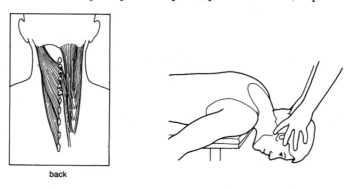

back

Figure 8–3 Manual neck lateral flexion
   Muscles developed: sternocleidomastoideus, scaleni

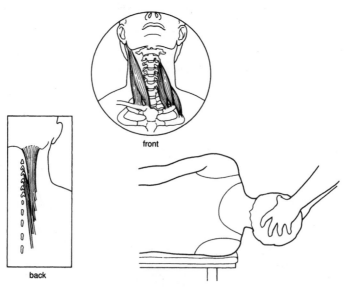

front

back

ply resistance to the side of your head as you attempt to bring your ear to your shoulder. Do this exercise on the right and left sides of your body.

Isometric Neck Exercises

You can increase neck strength by resisting neck movements with your hand and arm. Isometric neck exercises can overload neck muscles in flexion (chin toward chest), extension (pulling your head backward), and lateral flexion (bending your head to the right or left side).

◆   THE TECHNIQUE   For neck flexion, place the heel of the palm on your forehead and resist as you attempt to push your chin toward your chest. For neck extension, place the palm of your hand on the back of your head and resist as you attempt to push your head backward. For neck lateral flexion, place the palm of your hand on the side of your head and resist as you push your head to the side (do this exercise to the right and left sides).

Neck-Harness Exercises

Neck-harness exercises involve the same movements as manual-resistance neck exercises, except the resistance is provided by weights suspended from a neck harness rather than by a training partner. Neck harnesses are relatively inexpensive and can be purchased at almost any sporting goods store.

Neck exercises for the Universal Gym are identical to the neck-harness exercises presented in this chapter. The only difference between the two is that the Universal Gym neck harness is attached to the neck-conditioning station, whereas the free-weight neck harness is attached to weight plates. Weights attached to the neck harness provide resistance to the neck during neck flexion, extension, and lateral flexion.

◆   THE TECHNIQUE   Neck flexion (Figure 8–4): Wearing the neck harness, with weight suspended from the harness chain, lie on your back on a table. Allow your head to slowly roll backward, then pull the weight back up by moving your chin toward your chest. Make sure to hold the sides of the table with your hands so that you don't lose your balance.

Figure 8–4 Neck flexion with harness
Muscles developed: sternocleidomastoideus, scaleni

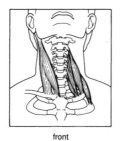

front

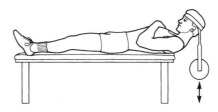

◆   THE TECHNIQUE   Neck extension (Figure 8–5): Wearing the neck harness, with weight suspended from the harness chair, stand with your knees bent and hands on your thighs. Slowly lower the weight with your neck as far as possible; then return to the starting position.

◆   THE TECHNIQUE   Neck lateral flexion: Wearing the neck harness, with weight suspended from the harness chain, lie on your side on a table or bench. Allow your head to slowly bend to the lower side, then pull the weight upward by moving your ear toward your higher shoulder. Do this exercise on the right and left sides of your body.

◆   THE TECHNIQUE   Neck lateral flexion, Universal Gym (Figure 8–6): Stand with the side of your face exposed to the neck machine. Put the harness on your head and attach the fastener to the neck-conditioning station. Stand far enough away from the machine so that you feel tension on the harness. Bend your head toward your outer shoulder.

Neck-Machine Exercises

Several equipment manufacturers make neck exercise machines that provide resistance during neck flexion, extension, and lateral flexion. Nautilus makes a neck-rotation machine, but few facilities have it. Working out on neck machines is probably superior to performing the manual or neck-harness methods, so use the machines if you have access to them.

Four-Way Neck Machines — Nautilus, Eagle

Four-way neck machines allow you to do neck flexion, extension, and lateral flexion. Each movement requires you to change your seating position. Do these exercises with your neck muscles, not your trunk.

Figure 8–5 Neck extension with harness
          Muscles developed: splenius capitus, splenius cervicus, trapezius

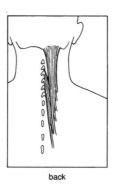

back

Figure 8–6 Lateral neck flexion, Universal Gym
         Muscles developed: sternocleidomastoideus, scaleni

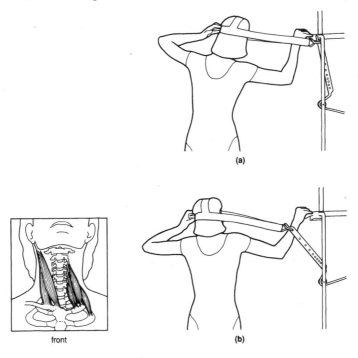

front   (b)

◆ **THE TECHNIQUE**   Flexion (Figure 8–7a): Adjust the seat so that the front of your forehead rests in the center of the two pads (starting position). Bend your head forward as far as possible; then return to the starting position.

◆ **THE TECHNIQUE**   Lateral flexion (Figure 8–7b): Adjust the seat so that the side of your head rests in the center of the two pads (starting position). Bend your head sideways toward your shoulder as far as possible; then return to the starting position. Do the exercise on the right and left sides of your head.

◆ **THE TECHNIQUE**   Extension (Figure 8–7c): Adjust the seat so that the back of your head rests in the center of the two pads (starting position). Bend your head backward as far as possible; then return to the starting position.

Figure 8–7 (a) Neck flexion (Eagle), (b) lateral flexion, (c) extension on Nautilus machine
Muscles developed, flexion (a): sternocleidomastoideus, scaleni
Muscles developed, lateral flexion (b): sternocleidomastoideus, scaleni
Muscles developed, extension (c): splenius capitus, splenius cervicus, trapezius

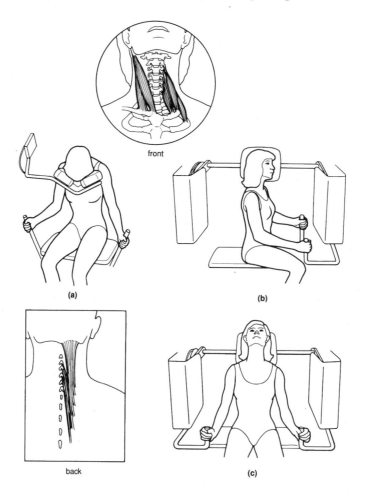

EXERCISES FOR THE UPPER BACK: THE TRAPS

In the upper back, the two most important muscles for movement are the trapezius and latissimus dorsi, which weight trainers refer to as the "traps" and "lats." Many exercises presented in this book develop the upper back, but the following exercises are good for specifically training the traps.

- ◆ Shoulder shrugs
- ◆ Nautilus neck and shoulder machine (a shoulder-shrug machine)
- ◆ Rowing exercises

The traps are also developed when you do overhead presses, upright rowing (see Chapter 6), and pulling exercises (e.g., cleans, snatches, and high pulls; see Chapter 10). If you are doing these exercises, you probably don't need to do additional exercise for this muscle.

Shoulder Shrugs

Shoulder shrugs can be done with a barbell or with commercially manufactured shoulder-shrug machines. Be careful not to cheat on this exercise—it's easy to let your legs initiate the movement.

◆   THE TECHNIQUE   In a standing position, hold a barbell with a pronated grip, hands shoulder-width apart, arms extended, and the weight resting below your waist (Figure 8–8). Without bending your elbows, lift ("shrug") your shoulders toward your head, rotate your shoulders back; then return to the starting position.

Shoulder Shrugs, Universal Gym

◆   THE TECHNIQUE   Remove the bench and use the bench-press station on the Universal Gym (Figure 8–9). Face the machine, grasp the handles using a pronated grip with arms extended, and lift the bar to your waist (starting position). Without bending your elbows, lift your shoulders toward your head, rotate your shoulders back; then return to the starting position.

Neck and Shoulder Machine (Shoulder Shrugs), Nautilus

The Nautilus neck and shoulder machine provides an excellent way to do shoulder shrugs because it is not limited by the strength of your grip (you don't hold onto a bar).

Figure 8–8 Shoulder shrugs
Muscles developed: trapezius, rhomboids, deltoid

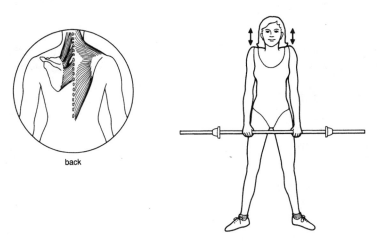

back

Figure 8–9 Shoulder shrugs, Universal Gym
Muscles developed: trapezius, rhomboids, deltoid

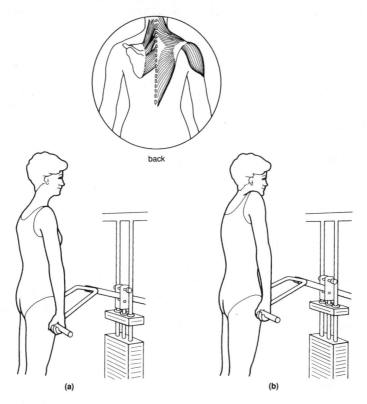

back

(a)   (b)

◆   THE TECHNIQUE   Sit facing the machine and place each forearm through the support pads with your palms down (starting position). With elbows flexed, shrug your shoulders toward your head; then return to the starting position (Figure 8–10).

Bent-Over Rowing

Upright rowing was described in Chapter 6 as a good shoulder exercise. In addition to working the major muscles of the upper back, bent-over rowing works the shoulders.

◆   THE TECHNIQUE   Bend at the waist with knees bent and arms extended, holding a barbell or dumbbell (Figure 8–11). Lift the weight to your chest; then return to the starting position. The shoulder blades should move together as the arms pull back; otherwise, the biceps do most of the work.

| CAUTION | ◆ | This exercise may place excessive pressure on your intervertebral disks, so don't do it if you have back trouble. |

Figure 8–10 Nautilus neck and shoulder (shoulder shrug) machine
Muscles developed: trapezius, rhomboids, deltoid

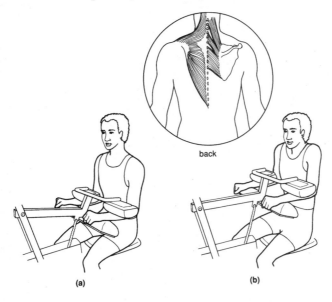

(a)   (b)

Figure 8–11 Bent-over rowing
Muscles developed: trapezius, rhomboids, posterior deltoid, biceps, latissimus dorsi

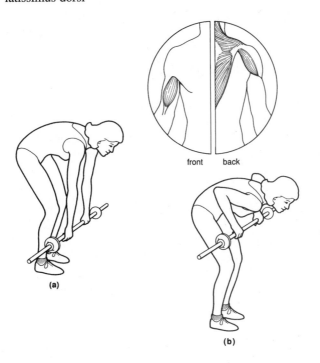

(a)

(b)

Figure 8–12 Bent-over rowing, Universal Gym
Muscles developed: trapezius, latissimus dorsi, posterior deltoid, biceps, rhomboids

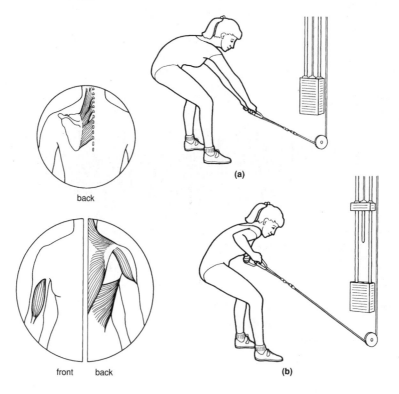

Bent-Over Rowing, Universal Gym

◆   THE TECHNIQUE   Using the low pulley station on the Universal Gym, face the machine and bend forward at the waist, keeping your back straight and knees bent (starting position). Stand far enough away from the machine so that your arms are extended (Figure 8–12). Using either the small bar or the handles, pull the bar toward your chest; then return to the starting position.

EXERCISES FOR THE UPPER BACK: THE LATS

The latissimus dorsi (the "lats") move the arms downward, backward, and inward. They are used in the tennis serve and when throwing a ball. A variety of exercises already discussed work the lats, including pullovers, the Nautilus pullover machine, parallel-bar dips, and bent-over rowing, but the following two exercises are particularly effective:

- ◆ Pull-ups (pull-ups, chin-ups, and behind-the-neck pull-ups)
- ◆ Lat pulls on lat machines

Pull-Ups

Pull-ups are extremely effective exercises for building the lats and other upper-body muscles. You can do them wherever you find a bar on which to pull yourself up — there are pull-up bars in any gymnasium or playground — or you can purchase one that can be mounted in a doorway. If you can't do this exercise at first, have a spotter hold you at the waist and assist you with the movement. And don't worry — you'll be able to do unassisted pull-ups in a short time.

◆   THE TECHNIQUE   Pull-ups (Figure 8–13a): Hang from a bar, elbows fully extended, using a pronated grip, with hands slightly more than shoulder width apart. Pull yourself up until your chin passes the bar; then return to the starting position. Do not swing your legs during this exercise, and be sure to fully extend your elbows after each repetition.

◆   THE TECHNIQUE   Chin-ups (Figure 8–13b): This exercise is identical to pull-ups except that you use a supinated grip. Chin-ups are easier, however, so they are a good exercise if you have difficulty performing the other forms of this exercise. Chin-ups are excellent for building the biceps.

Figure 8–13 (a) Pull-ups, (b) chin-ups, and (c) behind-the-neck pull-ups
         Muscles developed: latissimus dorsi, biceps

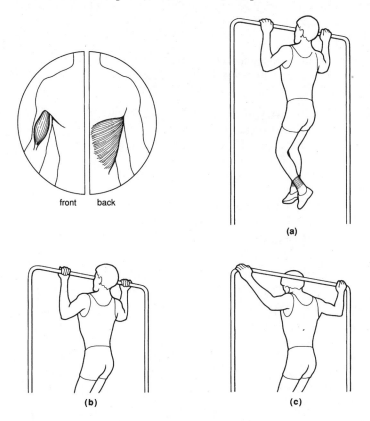

front   back

(a)

(b)   (c)

◆   THE TECHNIQUE   Behind-the-neck pull-ups (Figure 8–13c): This exercise places more stress on the lats and is much more difficult than the other kinds of pull-ups. Hang from a bar, using a pronated grip, with hands as far apart as possible. Pull yourself up until the back of your neck makes contact with the bar; then return to the starting position.

Lat Pulls on Universal, Nautilus, or Other Lat Machines

Lat pulls require the use of a lat machine. They are very similar to pull-ups except that you pull weights down instead of pulling your body weight up. They also develop the muscles on the front of your arm (biceps). To work the lats more, do the exercise using a wide grip; to work the biceps more, use a narrower grip.

◆   THE TECHNIQUE   From a seated or kneeling position, grasp the bar of the lat machine, with arms fully extended (Figure 8–14). Pull the weight down until it reaches the back of your neck; then return to the starting position.

CAUTION ◆   Take care not to touch your neck bones with the bar; you could injure them if you mistakenly bang them too hard.

As you get stronger, you may need a spotter to hold you down during the exercise because the weight you use may pull you up (Figure 8–15). The spotter should get behind you and place his or her hands firmly on your shoulders.

CAUTION ◆   Spotters must take great care to keep their head away from the bar; they can be seriously injured if the lifter suddenly lets go of the bar.

◆   THE TECHNIQUE   Lat-pull machine, Nautilus (Figure 8–16): Adjust the seat so that your arms can be fully extended. Strap yourself in with the seat belt, extend your arms, and grasp the handles of the small bar (starting position). Pull the bar to your collarbone; then return to the starting position.

Figure 8–14 Lat pulls
Muscles developed: latissimus dorsi, biceps

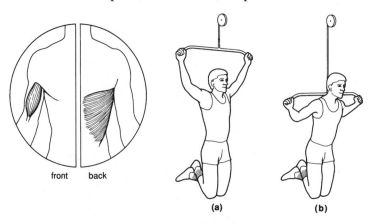

front   back

(a)   (b)

Figure 8–15 Spotting during lat-pull exercise

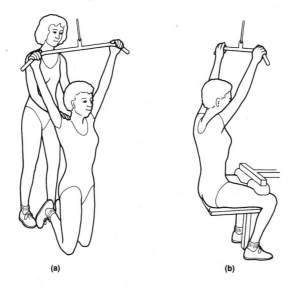

(a)   (b)

Figure 8–16 Lat pull, Nautilus
Muscles developed: latissimus dorsi, biceps

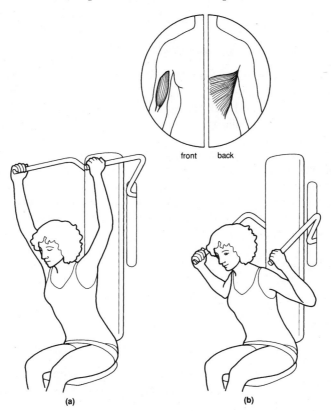

front   back

(a)   (b)

EXERCISES FOR THE LOWER BACK

More than 85 percent of the population has back pain at some time during their life. Some of this is due to poor strength and flexibility of the spinal muscles. An ideal exercise program for the lower back builds strong, flexible back muscles to help achieve optimal spinal alignment and minimize pressure on the spinal nerves. Unfortunately, the best exercises for strengthening the low-back muscles are often the same exercises that place the most stress on the spinal disks. Low-back muscles are well suited for maintaining an erect posture, but poorly suited for lifting heavy objects. Therefore, proper lifting techniques are absolutely essential when working the lower back. (These techniques were discussed in Chapter 5.)

Other factors important to a healthy back include strong abdominal and strong, flexible leg muscles. Regular aerobic exercise is also thought to help prevent back pain.

Four types of low-back exercises are discussed next:

- Isometric spine-extension exercises
- Specific low-back weight-training exercises
- Pelvic tilt
- Weight-training exercises having a secondary effect on the low-back muscles

No low-back program is right for everyone. If an exercise causes pain, stop doing it and seek professional advice. Circumstances change; an exercise that is inappropriate for you now may be all right 6 months from now after a period of conditioning.

Isometric Spine-Extension Exercises

The purpose of isometric extension exercises is to strengthen the low-back muscles so that they are better able to maintain spinal alignment. These exercises are very good for helping stabilize your spine, which most back experts feel is the key to a pain-free back. Two exercises in this category include unilateral spine extensions and bilateral spine extensions.

◆   THE TECHNIQUE   Unilateral spine extensions (Figure 8–17a): Balance on your right hand and knee. Extend your left leg to the rear, and reach forward with your left arm. Hold this position for 10 to 30 seconds. Repeat with your right leg and right arm. Start with 5 repetitions and advance to 15. You can make this exercise more difficult by attaching weights to your legs and arms. Ankle and wrist weights are inexpensive and can be purchased at any sporting goods store.

◆   THE TECHNIQUE   Bilateral spine extensions (Figure 8–17b): Balance on your right hand and left knee. Lift your right leg and left arm. Extend your leg to the rear, and reach to the front with your arm. Hold this position for 10 to 30 seconds. Repeat with the opposite arm and leg.

Low-Back Exercises

Weak back muscles are easily injured when you do squats and pulling exercises (e.g., cleans and snatches). So, if your weight-training program includes these exercises, it's a good idea

Figure 8–17 (a) Unilateral spine extensions, (b) bilateral spine extensions
Muscles developed: sacrospinalis, gluteus maximus

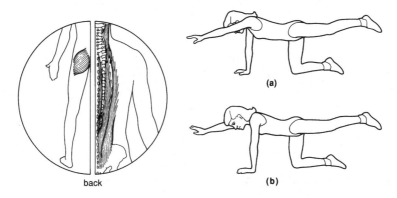

to add low-back exercises. Three popular ones are back extensions, the good-morning exercise, and the Nautilus back-extension machine.

CAUTION   ◆   Low-back weight-training exercises may subject the spinal disks to considerable pressure. If you suffer from low-back pain, these exercises may do more harm than good. Straight-leg dead lifts, although very popular, are not recommended at all.

Back extensions, Universal Gym or back-extension machine   Back extensions are also often called "back hyperextensions." However, it is not a good idea to extend too far backward—this could put excessive pressure on the spinal disks.

◆   THE TECHNIQUE   Lie face down on a back-extension bench with your upper body extending over the edge (Figure 8–18). Hang down as far as you can; then lift your torso until it is again aligned with your legs. You can do this exercise on a bench if you have a spotter holding your legs down.

The good-morning exercise   This is a particularly good accessory exercise to a program containing squats and pulling exercises.

◆   THE TECHNIQUE   Standing, place a barbell on your shoulders and flex your knees slightly (starting position). Bend at the waist while keeping your head up and spine rigid as much as possible; then return to the starting position (Figure 8–19). Do this exercise slowly and smoothly, and add weight very gradually. In general, do more repetitions (10 to 20) and use less weight than you normally would for other weight-training exercises.

Nautilus back-extension machine

◆   THE TECHNIQUE   Sit on the seat and place your upper legs under the large thigh-support pads, your back on the back roller pad, and your feet planted firmly on the platform (starting position). Placing your hands on your abdomen, extend backward until your back

Figure 8–18 Back extensions on Universal Gym
Muscles developed: sacrospinalis

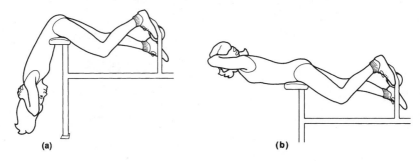

(a) (b)

Figure 8–19 The good-morning exercise
Muscles developed: sacrospinalis

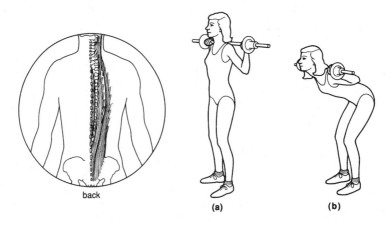

back

(a) (b)

is straight; then return to the starting position (Figure 8–20). Try to keep your spine rigid during the exercise.

Pelvic Tilt

This exercise strengthens the abdomen and low-back muscles and requires no equipment.

◆ THE TECHNIQUE   Lie on your back with knees bent and arms extended to the side (Figure 8–21). Tilt your pelvis under and try to flatten your lower back against the floor. Tighten your gluteal and abdominal muscles while you hold this position for 5 to 10 seconds. Don't hold your breath. Work up to 10 repetitions of this exercise. Pelvic tilts can also be done standing or leaning against a wall.

Exercises with a Secondary Effect on the Lower Back

Because the lower back is used to stabilize the upper body during many activities, almost all weight-training exercises stress the low-back muscles to a certain extent. Exercises such as squats, cleans, and snatches are particularly good at developing low-back strength.

Figure 8–20 Nautilus back-extension machine
Muscles developed: sacrospinalis

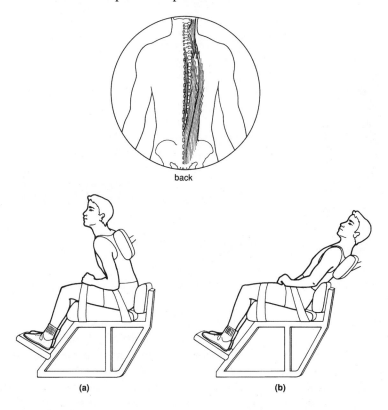

back

(a)   (b)

Figure 8–21 Pelvic tilt
Muscles developed: sacrospinalis, rectus abdominus

| CAUTION | ◆ | Because these lifts actively involve the back, it is particularly important to protect the back by wearing a weight-lifting belt and observing proper lifting techniques. |

CHAPTER

9 Developing the Abdominal Muscles

MOST PEOPLE WANT A FLAT STOMACH. WELL, HERE'S SOME GOOD NEWS AND SOME BAD news. No matter how much exercise you do, fat around the middle will remain unless you burn up more calories than you take in. There is no such thing as spot reducing—you can't exercise muscles and lose the fat lying over them.

Now, for the good news. The abdominal muscles are the major supporting structures of the abdomen. Unlike the legs and arms, which have large bones that provide structure, the abdomen has no bones. Strong muscles add support to the area and act like a biological girdle to "hold you in." If you strengthen the abdominal muscles, the area will look tighter, even though the fat may still be there.

The principal abdominal muscles include the rectus abdominis, which causes the trunk to bend or flex, and the obliques, which assist the rectus and allow you to rotate your trunk and bend to the side.

There are many abdominal exercises, but a number of these could injure the neck and low back and should be avoided. Dangerous abdominal exercises include Roman chair sit-ups (Figure 9–1a), straight-leg sit-ups (Figure 9–1b), double-leg lifts, and sit-ups with hands behind the head.

| CAUTION | ◆ | Roman chair sit-ups, straight-leg sit-ups, and double-leg lifts place excessive stress on the intervertebral disks. Doing sit-ups with hands behind the head could injure your neck. |

Doing a few sets of these dangerous exercises probably will not cause immediate injury. Doing them for many years could stress the disks, which eventually could lead to disk

Figure 9–1 Dangerous abdominal exercises

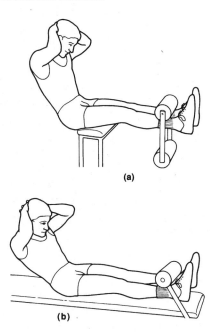

deterioration and chronic back and neck pain. The best practice is to avoid exercises that may cause problems.

Many exercises are effective for building the muscles of the trunk, including the following:

- Isometric abdominal exercise
- Crunches
- Sit-ups
- Nautilus abdominal machine
- Hanging knee raises
- Reverse beetles
- Nautilus hip-flexion machine
- Twists
- Nautilus rotary torso machine

ABDOMINAL AND HIP-FLEXOR EXERCISES

Isometric Abdominal Exercise

Perhaps you're not aware that you have your own built-in abdominal exercise machine. You can work on your abdominal muscles any time, anywhere.

◆   THE TECHNIQUE   To do the isometric abdominal exercise, simply tighten your abdominal muscles for 10 to 30 seconds. In other words, hold your stomach in. If you do this periodically during the day, you will notice a difference within a few weeks. But don't hold your breath while doing it, because this could restrict blood flow to the heart.

Crunches

Sports scientists have discovered that the abdominal muscles can get a tremendous workout by moving through a very small range of motion. You don't need to do full sit-ups to develop fully trained abdominals. Crunches have been found to be just as effective, and they place much less stress on the back.

◆   THE TECHNIQUE   Lie on your back on the floor (Figure 9–2). Place your feet on the floor or on a bench, or extend your legs up a wall. With arms folded across your chest, curl your trunk up and forward by raising your head and shoulders from the ground. Your back should remain stationary. Resistance can be increased by holding a weight plate on your chest.

Sit-Ups

Sit-ups are a basic exercise in almost everyone's program. Thirty years ago, sit-ups were done with straight legs. Scientists found that straight-leg sit-ups are hard on the back and exercise a large hip-flexor muscle group more than the abdominals. Holding your hands behind your head when doing sit-ups may cause neck injuries. Little of the exercise's value is lost by doing it with arms folded across the chest or hands touching the ears. If you insist on doing sit-ups with your hands behind your head, use your hands only to cradle your head—not to help you complete the exercise.

◆   THE TECHNIQUE   Lying on your back with knees bent, feet flat on the floor, and arms folded across the chest, bend at the waist and raise your head and shoulders toward your knees until your hands touch your thighs (Figure 9–3). Return to the starting position. You can modify this exercise to increase the stress on the obliques by twisting on the way up. As with crunches, the resistance can be increased by doing this exercise with weights.

Figure 9–2 Crunches (abdominal curls)
             Muscles developed: rectus abdominus

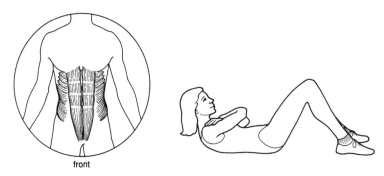

front

Figure 9–3   Sit-ups
Muscles developed: rectus abdominus, obliques

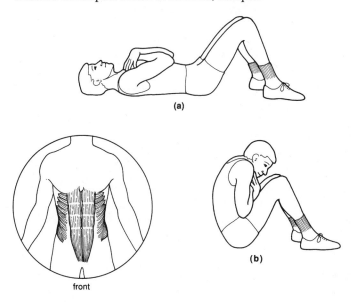

(a)

front

(b)

Slantboard Bent-Knee Sit-Ups, Universal Gym

Slantboard bent-knee sit-ups can be done on any slantboard made for doing sit-ups. A problem with this exercise is that it's difficult to bend your knees while doing it, particularly as the angle of the board increases. As with regular sit-ups, do not put your hands behind your head. (This is even more important when you're using a slantboard.)

◆   THE TECHNIQUE   Set the board at an angle that allows you to maintain bent knees throughout the exercise (Figure 9–4a). Start with no slant if you are unsure of your capabilities. With your hands folded across your chest, lie supine on the board, knees bent, and feet firmly anchored under the support cushions or belt (starting position). Bend at the waist and sit up. Twisting at the waist during this exercise will develop your abdominal oblique muscles (Figure 9–4b).

CAUTION   ◆   Be sure to do this exercise with your abdominal muscles — don't "rock" your body forward because you could injure your back. Never place your hands behind your head because of the possibility of neck injury.

Nautilus Abdominal Machine

The Nautilus abdominal machine looks very similar to its back machine, except you push forward instead of backward.

◆   THE TECHNIQUE   Adjust the seat so that the machine rotates at the level of your navel, the pad rests on your upper chest, and your feet can rest comfortably on the floor (starting position). Move your trunk forward as much as possible, then return to the starting position (Figure 9–5).

Hanging Knee Raises

This exercise is done hanging from a bar, between two bars, or on the hip-flexor station of the Universal Gym. It is a good exercise for the abdominal and hip-flexor muscles.

◆   THE TECHNIQUE   While hanging from a bar, bring your knees up toward your chest; then return to the starting position (Figure 9–6a, b).

◆   THE TECHNIQUE   Hip-flexor machine, Universal Gym: On the hip-flexor station of the Universal Gym, grasp the handles and rest your forearms on the pads (starting position). Draw your knees toward your chest, then return to the starting position (Figure 9–6c, d).

Reverse Beetles

This exercise got its name from the way weight trainers look when they do it — they resemble beetles that have been turned over on their back. By twisting as you do them, you can modify reverse beetles to increase the stress on the obliques.

Figure 9–4 Bent-knee sit-ups on Universal Gym slantboard
　　　　　 Muscles developed: rectus abdominus, obliques

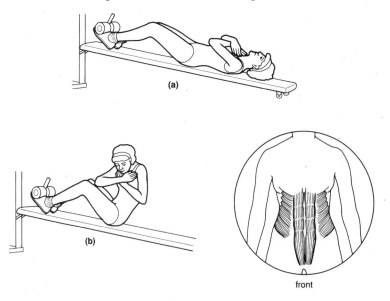

Figure 9–5 Nautilus abdominal machine
Muscles developed: rectus abdominus

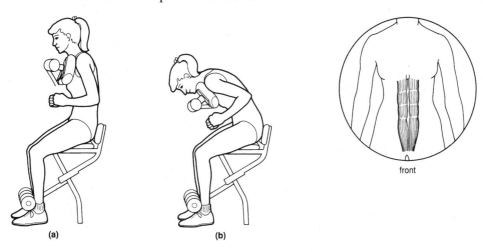

(a)   (b)   front

Figure 9–6 Hanging knee raises
Muscles developed: rectus abdominus, iliopsoas, quadriceps

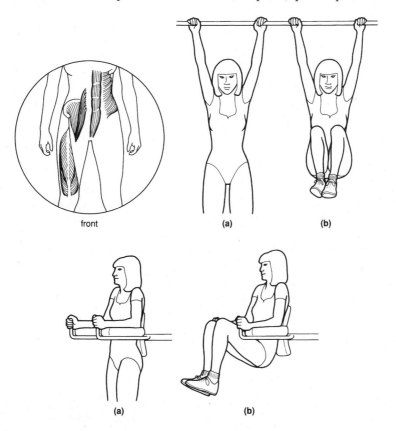

front   (a)   (b)

(a)   (b)

Figure 9–7 Reverse beetles
          Muscles developed: rectus abdominus, iliopsoas, quadriceps

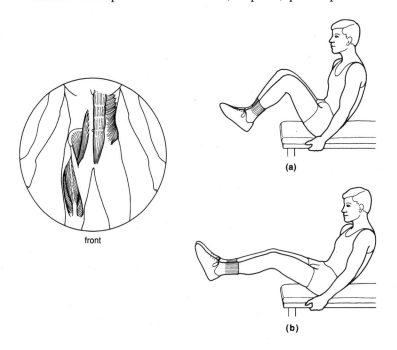

front

(a)

(b)

◆   THE TECHNIQUE   From a seated position on a bench, curl your trunk by bringing knees and shoulders together (Figure 9–7). Then straighten your legs and move your shoulders backward.

Hip-Flexion Machine, Nautilus

This hip-flexion exercise mainly strengthens the iliopsoas muscle, a hip flexor. However, the abdominal muscles work by stabilizing the trunk, so they get a good workout too. This exercise has many of the same effects as the hanging knee raises and reverse beetles.

◆   THE TECHNIQUE   Sit in the machine and fasten the belt across the middle of your thighs (Figure 9–8). Then lie on your back with your head resting on the bench and grab the handles behind your head (starting position). Bring your knees to your chest; then return to the starting position.

EXERCISES FOR THE OBLIQUES

Twists

Twists are a great way to exercise the obliques. But remember, exercising specific body parts will only help hold in the fat, not get rid of it. It may look better, but it is still there. This exercise may not be a good idea for people who have back pain.

Figure 9–8 Nautilus hip-flexion machine
   Muscles developed: rectus abdominus, iliopsoas, quadriceps

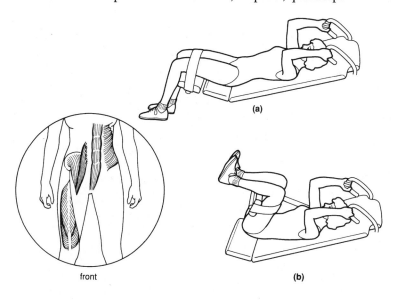

front   (b)

Figure 9–9 Twists
   Muscles developed: rectus abdominus, obliques

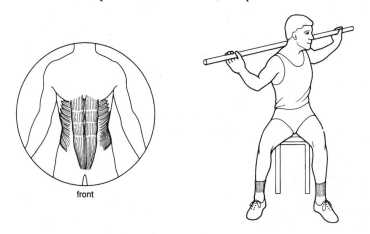

front

◆   THE TECHNIQUE   From either a seated or standing position, place a pole on your shoulders and rotate as far as possible, first to the left and then to the right (Figure 9–9). Later, you can use a barbell with weights to get added resistance. If you are more interested in definition than size (as most people are), do many repetitions rather than use a lot of weight.

CAUTION   ◆   Twisting exercises can cause back pain in some people—exercise with caution.

Figure 9–10 Rotary torso machine, Nautilus
       Muscles developed: internal and external obliques, rectus abdominus

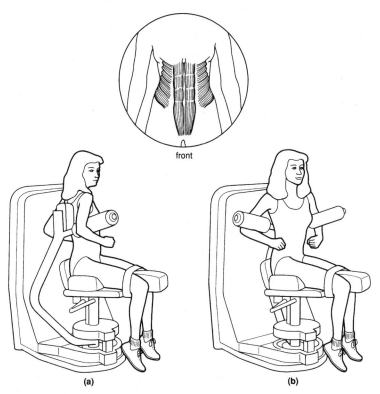

front

(a)   (b)

Rotary Torso Machine, Nautilus

The rotary torso machine is a "high-tech" twist machine. There are two sides to it—one to rotate your trunk clockwise and the other to work your trunk counterclockwise.

◆   THE TECHNIQUE   Sit on the seat (adjusted to the right side) and wrap your arms around the handles (Figure 9–10). Pull with your right arm and twist your trunk toward your left side. After completing your repetitions, adjust the seat to the left, sit on the seat, wrap your arms around the handles and pull with your left arm, twisting your trunk toward your right side.

10 Developing the Lower Body

THE LEG MUSCLES ARE THE LARGEST AND MOST POWERFUL IN THE BODY. POWERFUL MOVE-ments in most sports are initiated with the leg and hip muscles. For example, golfers and tennis players start with movement in their legs and finish the movement with their upper body. Those failing to use the lower body effectively, relying instead on the weaker and more fragile upper-body muscles, perform inefficiently and are more prone to injury.

Figure 10–1 shows the basic athletic position used in sports such as tennis, racquetball, and volleyball. The legs are bent and the center of gravity is low. The person can easily move in any direction and has good stability. Movement is much easier and more effective if the lower-body muscles are strong and powerful.

Figure 10–1 Basic athletic position

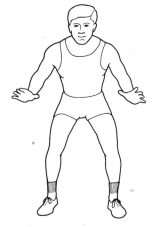

This chapter discusses exercise for developing strength, power, and muscle shape in the lower body: multijoint exercises, accessory leg-strengthening exercises, and advanced lifts. You will have stronger, more defined legs if you include some of these exercises in your program.

MULTIJOINT LOWER-BODY EXERCISES

Multijoint exercises involve movement in two or more joints. Squats and leg presses are multijoint exercises that develop strength in the lower body, which can improve performance in most sports. They also increase strength, to a certain extent, in the back and abdominal muscles. Exercises included in this chapter are

- Squats
- Power-rack squats
- Smith-machine squats
- Front squats
- Hack squats
- Wall squats (phantom chair)
- Leg presses (Universal Gym and Nautilus)
- Lunges

Squats

Many people avoid squats because of reports that deep knee bends overstretch the knee ligaments. In fact, you can squat very low before the knee ligaments are stretched significantly. Good form is essential in this lift. Beginners often use too much weight; consequently, they bend their back excessively during the lift and sometimes injure themselves.

◆ THE TECHNIQUE   Most experts recommend using a weight-lifting belt when doing squats. Begin the exercise standing with your feet shoulder-width apart and toes pointed slightly outward. Rest the bar on the back of your shoulders, your hands holding the bar in that position (Figure 10–2). Keep your head up and lower back straight. Squat down (under control) until your thighs are approximately parallel with the floor and gluteals are about 1 inch below the knee. Drive upward toward the starting position, keeping your back in a fixed position throughout the exercise. A general strategy for this lift is to go down slowly and up quickly.

| CAUTION | ◆ Never "bounce" at the bottom of the squat—this could injure the ligaments of your knee. |

Safety should be of primary concern. A good squat rack is an important prerequisite. The rack should be sturdy and adjustable for people of different heights. Some racks have a safety bar at the bottom that can be used if the lift cannot be completed. Two spotters are

Figure 10–2 The squat

Muscles developed: quadriceps, gluteus maximus, sacrospinalis, hamstrings

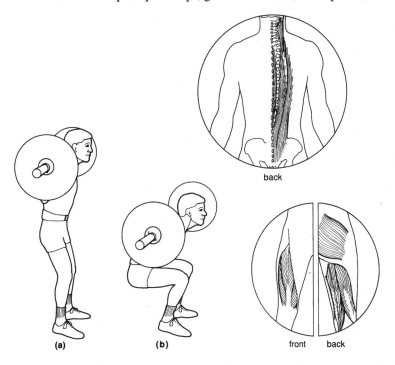

also required—one standing on each side of the lifter, prepared to assist in case the person fails to complete the lift. Some people wrap their knees and use weight-lifting boots to provide added support.

You can do many variations to this exercise to increase squatting power, such as power-rack squats and bench squats. Because of the high risk of injury, I do not recommend bench squats.

CAUTION ◆ Bench squats can be dangerous: You may unintentionally slam down on the bench during the exercise and injure your spine.

Power-Rack Squats

Power-rack squats allow you to use the power rack to overcome sticking points in the range of motion of the squat exercise. As with the power-rack bench press described in Chapter 6, you select three positions along the range of motion and work out at each one.

◆   THE TECHNIQUE   Place the bar on the first pair of pegs so that it rests on your shoulders and your thighs are nearly parallel to the ground (Figure 10–3). Push the weight upward until you are standing upright. After your workout at the first position, move the pegs so that the bar lies in the middle of the range of motion. Repeat the exercise sequence. Finally, move the pegs so that the bar travels only a few inches during the exercise. At this

Figure 10–3 Power-rack squat

Muscles developed: quadriceps, gluteus maximus, sacrospinalis, hamstrings

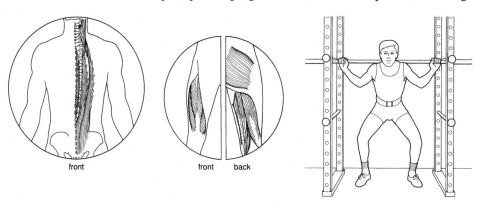

front   front   back

peg stop, you will be capable of handling much more weight than you can from the parallel squat position.

Smith-Machine Squats

The Smith machine was described in Chapter 6. This exercise machine is excellent for doing squats because it helps keep your back in a good position when doing the exercise. Perform squats on the Smith machine in the same way you do them with free weights. If you are experiencing back pain, step forward slightly when doing the exercise so that you are leaning slightly into the bar. This will take pressure off your low back.

Front Squats

The front squat is a variation of the squat and is used mainly in training programs of Olympic-style weight lifters. This lift isolates the leg muscles better than the regular squat, because the back cannot be used as much to assist in the movement; consequently, you cannot lift as much weight in this exercise.

◆   THE TECHNIQUE   Standing with your feet shoulder-width apart and toes pointed slightly outward, hold the bar on your chest and squat down until your gluteals are 1 inch below the knee (Figure 10–4). Do this exercise with good control because you can easily lose your balance. Stability can be improved by using weight-lifting shoes.

Hack Squats

Hack squats isolate the thigh muscles more than squats because they force you to keep your back straighter—even more so than during front squats. This exercise is generally used as an auxiliary to squats rather than as the primary leg exercise.

◆   THE TECHNIQUE   In a standing position, hold a barbell behind you with your arms fully extended down so that the weight rests on the back of your thighs (Figure 10–5). Slowly squat until the weight nearly reaches the ground, then push up to the starting position.

Figure 10–4 Front squats
Muscles developed: quadriceps, gluteus maximus, sacrospinalis, deltoid (support), hamstrings

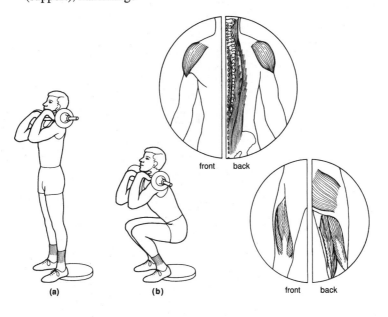

Figure 10–5 Hack squats
Muscles developed: quadriceps, gluteus maximus, sacrospinalis, hamstrings

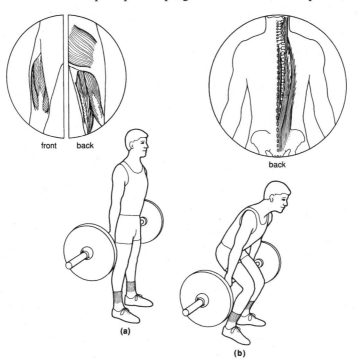

Figure 10–6 Wall squats

Wall Squats (Phantom Chair)

The wall squat is an excellent exercise for your thigh muscles that requires no equipment. It is a particularly good exercise for ski conditioning.

◆   THE TECHNIQUE   Lean against a wall and bend your knees as though you were sitting in a chair (Figure 10–6). Support your weight with your legs. Begin by holding that position for 5 to 10 seconds. Build up to a minute or more.

CAUTION   ◆   Wall squats may cause pain under or around the kneecap in some people. If you experience kneecap pain, particularly the day after doing the exercise, don't do this exercise, or decrease the time you stay in the squat position.

Leg Presses, Universal Gym and Nautilus

Leg presses are done on leg-press exercise machines and can be substituted for squats. They are safer and more convenient to do than squats because they don't involve handling weight, place less stress on the back, and don't require a spotter. Leg presses, however, are less effective than squats for developing strength in the quadriceps, gluteals, and hamstrings.

Figure 10–7 Leg press on Universal Gym
Muscles developed: quadriceps, gluteus maximus, hamstrings

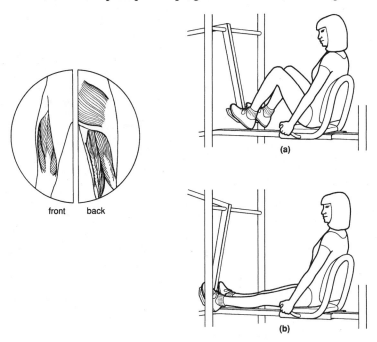

front   back

(a)

(b)

◆ **THE TECHNIQUE** Universal Gym: Adjust seat so that knees are bent at a 60- to 90-degree angle (Figure 10–7). Grasp the side handlebars and push with your legs until your knees are fully extended. Return to the starting position. Don't bang the weights as you finish the repetition.

◆ **THE TECHNIQUE** Nautilus Duo squat machine: Adjust the seat so that your knees are bent approximately 90 degrees (Figure 10–8). Sit with your shoulders under the shoulder pads, feet on the foot pedals, hands on the side handles, and legs fully extended (starting position). Bend your left leg 90 degrees; then forcefully extend it. Repeat with your right leg. Then alternate between left and right leg.

◆ **THE TECHNIQUE** Nautilus leg-press machine: Adjust the seat so that your knees are bent approximately 90 degrees when beginning the exercise (starting position). Push out forcefully until your knees are fully extended; then return to the starting position (Figure 10–9).

Lunges

Lunges are a great exercise for the quadriceps (front of thigh), gluteus maximus (buttocks), and, to a lesser extent, the calf and lower-back muscles.

Figure 10–8 Nautilus Duo squat machine
Muscles developed: quadriceps, gluteus maximus, hamstrings

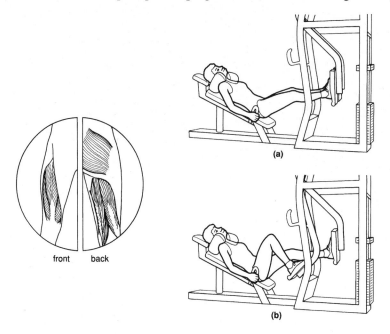

Figure 10–9 Nautilus leg-press machine
Muscles developed: quadriceps, gluteus maximus, hamstrings

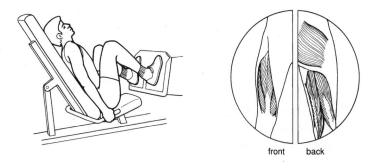

◆   THE TECHNIQUE   Stand with your feet shoulder-width apart and the bar resting on the back of your shoulders, with your hands holding the bar in that position (Figure 10–10). Lunge forward with one leg, bending it until the thigh is parallel to the floor. Repeat the exercise using the other leg. Keep your back and head as straight as possible, and maintain control while performing the exercise.

Isokinetic Squat Machines

The high-speed squat machine is a relatively new product. These machines are constructed so that resistance is added to the movement when you are traveling relatively fast. They present a tremendous risk of injury and have no place in the weight room.

Figure 10–10 Lunges

Muscles developed: quadriceps, gluteus maximus, hamstrings

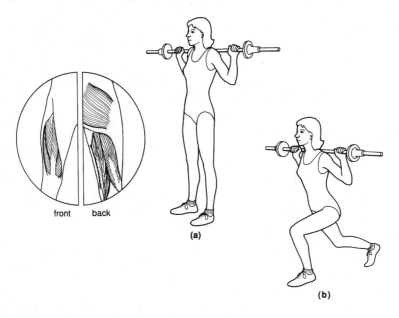

front   back

(a)

(b)

CAUTION   ◆   Sudden loading of the spine at high speeds may cause severe damage to the intervertebral disks. High-speed squat machines are not recommended.

AUXILIARY EXERCISES FOR THE LOWER BODY

Several accessory exercises for the lower body isolate distinct muscle groups, such as the quadriceps, hamstrings (back of thigh), and calf. Auxiliary exercises include

- ◆ Knee extensions (leg extensions)
- ◆ Knee flexions (leg curls)
- ◆ Heel raises
- ◆ Heel raises on Universal Gym
- ◆ Calf machine (multiexercise machine), Nautilus

Knee Extensions (Leg Extensions)

Knee extensions are done on a knee-extension machine. Most gyms, including Nautilus and Universal, have these machines. Knee extensions are excellent for building the quadriceps muscle group and are good for supplementing squats or leg presses in the general program.

Doing knee extensions with weighted boots is not recommended, because it may strain the ligaments of the knee.

CAUTION ◆ Knee extensions may cause kneecap pain in some people. (See "Kneecap Pain" in Chapter 2.) These exercises, particularly if done through a full range of motion, increase pressure on the kneecap and cause pain. If you have pain in your kneecaps, check with an orthopedic specialist before doing this exercise.

Doing knee extensions during the last 20 degrees of the range of motion (just before the knee is fully extended) builds up the muscle that tends to draw the kneecap toward the center of the joint. This exercise is often prescribed for people who have kneecap pain. The Lumex Company, which makes Eagle exercise equipment, makes a knee-extension machine that allows you to restrict the motion done during the exercise. The Eagle knee-extension machine is available in many health clubs.

◆ THE TECHNIQUE   Sit on the knee-extension bench and place your shins on the knee-extension pads (Figure 10–11). Extend your knees until they are straight; then return to the starting position.

◆ THE TECHNIQUE   Universal Gym knee-extension station: This exercise is done as described above. Resistance can be supplied via a cable stretching underneath the bench and connecting to a weight stack, or weights can be loaded on a peg attached to the front of the machine.

◆ THE TECHNIQUE   Nautilus knee-extension machine: This machine is similar to those described above except that the seat can be adjusted for differences in leg length.

Knee Flexions (Leg Curls)

Knee flexions, more commonly known as leg curls, require the use of a leg-curl machine. Nautilus and Universal Gym make these machines, as do other manufacturers. Instructions

Figure 10–11 Knee extensions
Muscles developed: quadriceps

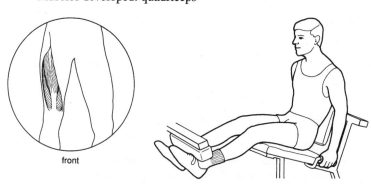

front

Figure 10–12 Knee flexions (leg curls)
Muscles developed: hamstrings

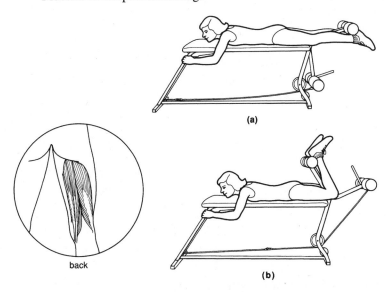

(a)

back

(b)

for this exercise are similar for most leg-curl machines. This exercise develops the hamstrings, the muscles on the back of the thighs.

Most sports build the quadriceps muscles, but few work on the hamstrings. Because injuries can be caused by imbalances between muscles, it is important to work on your hamstrings in addition to your quadriceps.

◆   THE TECHNIQUE   Lie on your stomach, resting the pads of the machine just below your calf muscles (Figure 10–12). Flex your knees until they approach your buttocks; then return to the starting position. Because the hamstrings are weaker than the quadriceps, you will be unable to handle as much weight on this exercise as on the knee-extension machine.

Heel Raises

Heel raises strengthen the calf muscles — the soleus, gastrocnemius, and plantaris — and the Achilles tendon, which connects the calf muscles to the heel. These exercises can be done anywhere there is a step or block of wood; they do not necessarily require weights.

◆   THE TECHNIQUE   Standing on the edge of a stair or block of wood with a barbell resting on your shoulders, slowly lower your heels as far as possible; then raise them until you are up on your toes (Figure 10–13). The calf muscles are very strong and require much resistance to increase their size and strength. You can add calf exercises at the end of your squat or leg-press routine. Do some heel raises after your last repetition.

Most gyms have some kind of calf exercise machine. Usually the machines are safer and easier to work with — you generally don't have to handle weights or worry about balance while carrying a lot of weight — and therefore are more effective than doing heel raises.

Figure 10–13 Heel raises
Muscles developed: gastrocnemius, soleus, plantaris

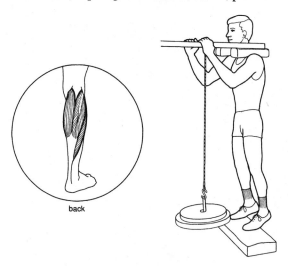

back

Heel Raises on Universal Gym

Heel raises can be conveniently done on the leg-press station of the Universal Gym immediately after doing leg presses.

◆   THE TECHNIQUE   Sit in the leg-extension station and fully extend your legs (starting position). Press down with your toes and lift your heels; then return to the starting position (Figure 10–14). You can work different portions of the calf muscles by pointing your feet straight ahead, inward, and outward.

Calf Machine (Multiexercise Machine), Nautilus

The Nautilus multiexercise machine can also be used to do pull-ups and bar dips.

◆   THE TECHNIQUE   Put the belt around your waist, attach it to the weight ring, and step up on the first step of the machine (starting position). Lift your heels and press up on your toes; then return to the starting position (Figure 10–15).

ADVANCED LIFTS

Popular with serious weight trainers, the advanced lifts are complex exercises that take a considerable amount of time to learn. They are very valuable because they develop strength from the basic athletic position (see Figure 10–1) and help improve strength and power for many sports. Advanced lifts include the following:

◆ Power cleans
◆ High pulls
◆ Dead lifts

Figure 10–14 Heel raises on Universal Gym leg-press station
Muscles developed: gastrocnemius, soleus, plantaris

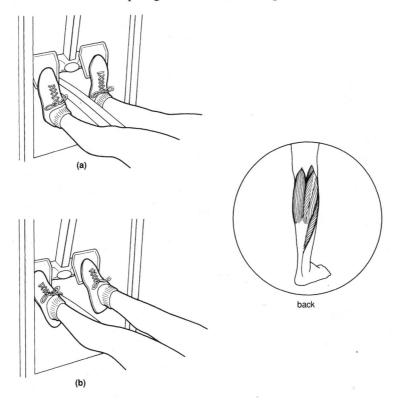

Figure 10–15 Heel raises on Nautilus multiexercise machine
Muscles developed: gastrocnemius, soleus, plantaris

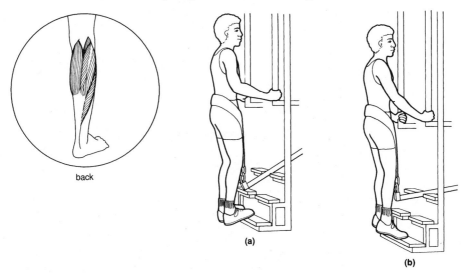

Figure 10–16   Power cleans

Muscles developed: quadriceps, gluteus maximus, trapezius, deltoids, sacrospinalis, hamstrings

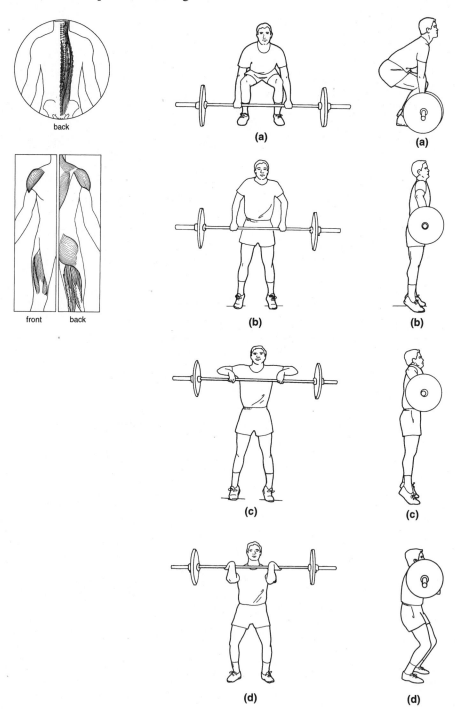

Power Cleans and High Pulls

The power clean is used to get the weight to the starting position for the overhead-press exercise (see "Overhead Press" in Chapter 6). It is an important exercise in the program of strength–speed athletes such as throwers, football players, multievent athletes (e.g., decathletes and heptathletes), and volleyball and basketball players.

◆   THE TECHNIQUE   Place the bar on the floor in front of your shins (Figure 10–16). Keep your feet approximately 2 feet apart. Using a pronated grip, grasp the bar with your hands at shoulder-width and squat, keeping your arms and back straight and your head up. Pull the weight up past your knees to your chest while throwing your hips forward and shoulders back. After pulling the weight as high as you can, bend the knees suddenly and catch the bar on your chest at a level just above your collarbone. Stand up straight with the bar at chest level. Return the bar to the starting position. The main power for this exercise should come from your hips and legs. Think of the middle phase of the lift as a vertical jump—this makes you drive up the weight with your legs, rather than your arms.

Variations of this lift include the high pull (Figure 10–17), squat clean, and split clean. The high pull is identical to the power clean except that you don't turn the bar over at the top of the lift and catch it at your chest. This procedure allows you to handle more weight and place less stress on your wrists and forearms. The squat clean and split clean, which are beyond the scope of this book, are used in Olympic weight lifting (a form of

Figure 10–17 High pull
Muscles developed: quadriceps, gluteus maximus, trapezius, deltoids, sacrospinalis, hamstrings

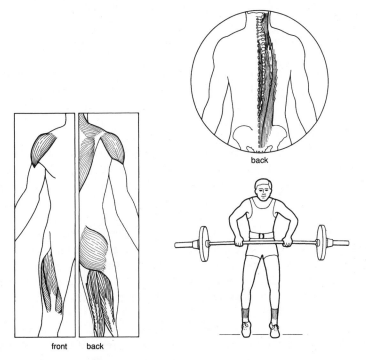

front   back

back

Figure 10–18 Dead lift
Muscles developed: quadriceps, gluteus maximus, trapezius, deltoids, sacrospinalis, hamstrings

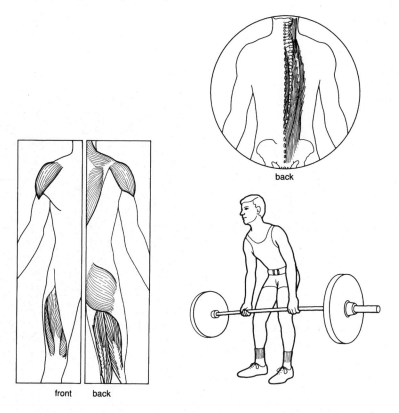

back

front   back

competitive weight lifting) and take a long time to learn. The snatch (an Olympic lift) is another pulling exercise that is extremely difficult for the novice to master.

Dead Lifts

The dead lift is one of the three power lifts (a weight-lifting competition event; the other two power lifts are the bench press and squat). It is an excellent exercise for the legs, buttocks, and back. Because it is possible to handle a great deal of weight in this exercise, it is critical that proper form be maintained to avoid back injury.

◆   THE TECHNIQUE   Place the bar on the floor in front of your shins (Figure 10–18). Keep your feet approximately shoulder-width apart. Using a dead-lift grip (see "Grips" in Chapter 5), grasp the bar at shoulder-width and squat down, keeping your arms and back straight and your head up. Pull the weight past your knees until you are in a fully erect position. Return the weight to the floor under control, being careful to bend only your knees and maintain a straight back.

Dead lifts can also be done on the bench-press station of the Universal Gym (Figure 10–19). Place a box (the kind used for step tests) in front of the bench-press station.

Figure 10–19 Dead lift on Universal Gym
Muscles developed: quadriceps, gluteus maximus, trapezius, deltoids, sacrospinalis, hamstrings

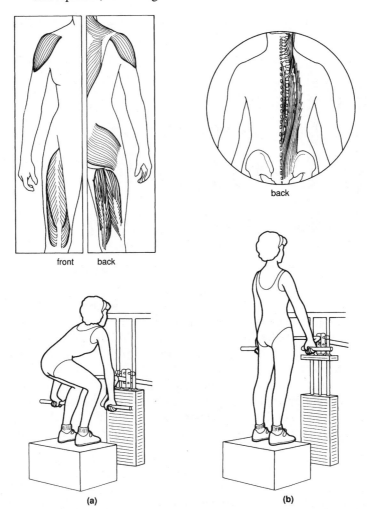

front   back

back

(a)   (b)

Grasp the handles with either a pronated or a dead-lift grip, with your hands shoulder-width apart. Squat down, keeping your arms and back straight and your head up. Pull the weight past your knees until you are in a fully erect position. Return to the starting position under control, without banging the weights on the weight stack and being careful to bend only your knees and to maintain a straight back.

11 Exercises to Develop Speed and Power

MANY PEOPLE LIFT WEIGHTS TO IMPROVE PERFORMANCE IN SPORTS. THEY BELIEVE THAT increased strength developed in the weight room will make them run faster, jump higher, and throw further. As examples, football players lift weights to block and tackle more forcefully; skiers, to edge their skis better; and tennis players, to hit the ball harder and move with more authority across the court.

In most sports, however, power is much more important than strength. Power is force you can exert rapidly. Power allows basketball players to make stellar leaps, pitchers to throw flaming fastballs, and golfers to hit booming drives. Unfortunately, the strength you gain in the weight room doesn't transfer automatically to more powerful movements in sports.

HOW TO IMPROVE POWER FOR SPORTS

Power is determined by the strength of your muscles, how fast your nervous system can activate your muscles, and muscle coordination. These processes are related—you can't become powerful without addressing each one. For example, simply increasing your bench press (1 repetition maximum) by 20 pounds may not help you throw a ball further. Your nervous system has to learn to use the new muscle strength in the throw.

For powerful motions, you must turn on your muscles quickly. Weight training will improve power. However, plyometric and speed exercises that train your neuromuscular system are better for developing power than weight training alone. These exercises force the neuromuscular system to move quickly. They also use your muscles' natural elasticity to produce more power. The ideal power-development program includes a combination of sports practice, speed and plyometric exercises, and weight training.

Plyometrics and Speed Exercises

As discussed in Chapter 2, groups of muscles and nerves form motor units. Your body uses small, slow motor units to lift light objects and perform ordinary movements, such as standing and sitting. You use larger and faster motor units for rapid, powerful movements, such as sprinting or jumping. Because most sports require maximum effort at least part of the time, developing fitness in the large motor units is very important.

A basic principle of sports physiology is that *a motor unit is trained in proportion to its recruitment.* This means you can improve your capacity for powerful movements only if you train the motor units used during the activity. To improve power for sports, overload your muscles at high speeds.

Sports movements use many muscles and joints at the same time. For example, jumping requires a coordinated action of muscles that move the ankle, knee, and hip joints, as well as many other joints in the upper body and spine. Most weight-training exercises overload muscles that move only one or two joints. Although weight-training exercises build muscle, they don't train the muscles to work in coordinated muscle movements. Plyometric and speed exercises overload muscles in a way similar to that in which muscles work during sports movements.

INJURY RISK OF POWER EXERCISES

Any high-intensity sport or exercise increases the risk of injury because you push your tissues closer to their breaking point. When doing plyometric and speed exercises, start gradually and progress slowly. If any pain persists after doing the exercise, modify the program by doing fewer sets and repetitions of the exercise, fewer exercises, or avoiding the advanced, high-impact exercises.

The intensity of plyometric and speed exercises ranges from simple bounces (jumping rapidly in place) to box jumping (jumping up and down from a box or bench). Start with the basic exercises and progress slowly to the more advanced movements. Don't advance until you can do the exercises without postexercise pain. If you progress slowly, you won't get hurt and will become faster and more powerful in sports.

BASIC SPEED AND POWER EXERCISES

Hundreds of speed and power exercises exist. This chapter introduces some basic exercises that will help you improve speed and power. For a more comprehensive discussion of this training technique, read specific books on plyometrics, such as *Jumping into Plyometrics* by Donald Chu.

An important principle of these exercises is when you complete 1 repetition, begin the next rep *immediately*. This overloads your muscles and trains your nervous system. For most of the following exercises, start with 1 set of 5 reps and progress to 3–5 sets of 10 reps.

CAUTION ◆ Always maintain control of your spine when doing plyometric and speed exercises. Try to direct forces through the length of the spine rather than across it. This will help you avoid back injuries.

Lower-Body Exercise

Although the following exercises develop power mainly in the lower body, they also develop coordination between upper- and lower-body muscles for whole-body power movements.

Ankle bounce   The ankle bounce is a simple plyometric exercise that develops power mainly in the calf muscles.

◆ THE TECHNIQUE   From a standing position, hands on hips, and knees slightly flexed, jump off the ground using mainly the muscles of your calves and feet (Figure 11–1). Try to "bounce" as quickly as possible when performing the exercise.
  Variation: Single-leg ankle bounce. Same as above, except with one leg at a time.

Squat jump   The squat jump is a basic exercise that should be a cornerstone of any program designed to develop jumping and lower-body power. This type of leg power is important in all sprint–speed sports.

Figure 11–1 Ankle bounce

◆   THE TECHNIQUE   Standing with weight on the balls of your feet, squat until your thighs are 3–4 inches above **parallel** (Figure 11–2). Jump up vigorously, fully extending your ankle, knee, and hip joints. As in all plyometric exercises, when you land, *immediately* repeat the exercise. During the exercise, rotate your arms forward in a circle.

Variation: Single-leg squat jumps. Same as above, except use one leg at a time (Figure 11–3). This is an advanced exercise and should be attempted only after you have first adapted to the basic exercises.

Figure 11–2 Squat jump

Figure 11–3 Single-leg squat jumps

Figure 11–4 Double-leg tuck jump

Double-leg tuck jump   The double-leg tuck jump is a more difficult variation of the squat jump.

◆   THE TECHNIQUE   Standing with weight on the balls of your feet, squat until your thighs are 3–4 inches above parallel. Jump up vigorously, fully extending your ankle, knee, and hip joints. As you complete the jump but are still in the air, draw (tuck) your knees vigorously toward your chest (Figure 11–4). *Move your knees to your chest, not your chest toward your knees.* Your arms use a "delayed rotation" movement to help you gain full lower-body extension. During the jump phase, your arms rotate upward to help you gain momentum. Delay the downward rotation of your arms as you tuck your knees to your chest. As you release your knees and descend to the ground, move your arms downward in preparation for the next jump.

Split (pike) jump

◆   THE TECHNIQUE   Standing with weight on the balls of your feet, squat until your thighs are 3–4 inches above parallel. Jump up vigorously, fully extending your ankle, knee, and hip joints. As you complete the jump but are still in the air, extend your legs into a split position (Figure 11–5). Use the "delayed rotation" arm movement described for tuck jumps.

Spin (360°) jump   The spin jump develops power for trunk rotation as well as for lower-body extension.

◆   THE TECHNIQUE   Standing with weight on the balls of your feet, squat until your thighs are 6–8 inches above parallel. Jump up vigorously, fully extending your ankle, knee, and hip joints. As you complete the jump but are still in the air, drive your arms and rotate your torso to one side so that you make a 360-degree turn in the air (Figure 11–6). Alternate between right and left turns. At first, if you can't do a full 360-degree turn, start with a quarter turn, gradually increasing it until you can complete the exercise.

Figure 11–5 Split (pike) jump

Figure 11–6 Spin (360°) jump

Ice skater   The ice-skater exercise develops lateral leg power and helps stabilize the back against lateral (shear) forces.

◆   THE TECHNIQUE   From a standing position, with your weight placed on the inside of the feet, extend with your legs and arms and jump to the right, using a speed-skating motion (Figure 11–7). Do the movement with your lower body; do not allow your trunk to sway in the direction of the skate. One repetition of this exercise is a jump to the left and to the right.
    Variations:

◆   Sand ice skaters. Same as above, except do the exercise in the sand (i.e., long-jump pit).

Figure 11–7 Ice-skater exercise

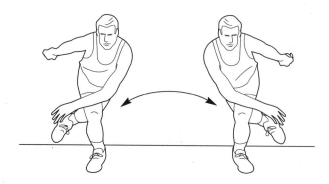

♦ Slide-board ice skater. Same as above, except do the exercise on a slide board. Slide boards are available commercially, or you can make one by building a wooden frame around a Formica board sprayed with silicon.

Repetitive leaps

♦ THE TECHNIQUE   From a standing position, flex your knees and hips slightly and draw your arms slightly behind your back (Figure 11–8). Jump forward vigorously by fully extending your ankles, knees, hips, and arms. When you land, jump again immediately. Begin with 2–3 jumps and progress to 5–10 jumps.

Variations:

♦ Single-leg jumps: Same exercise as above, except use only one leg at a time.

♦ Double-leg jumps over hurdles: Place small hurdles 3–5 feet apart and jump over them using the technique described above. This is an advanced exercise.

♦ Zigzag jumps over cones: Place 3–5 small cones 2 feet apart, with cones displaced by 2–3 feet. Jump over each cone as rapidly as possible.

♦ Single-leg zigzag jumps.

Box jumping   Box jumping should be attempted only after you have adapted to more basic exercises. Start with a small box or step about 0.3 meter (1 foot) high. At first, you need only one box; later, you will need several boxes in a row so that you can jump from one box to the ground to the next box and so on.

♦ THE TECHNIQUE   Box jumping should begin with low-impact jumps from a low box. An example of a conservative progression includes the following:

1. *Step-downs:* Step off a low box with either leg (Figure 11–9a). Land on both feet, placed shoulder-width apart. Flex the knees and hips slightly as you land.

2. *Step-down, jump-up:* Step off the box, land on both feet, absorbing the impact by flexing your knees and hips; then jump up, fully extending

Figure 11–8 Repetitive leaps

Figure 11–9a Step-downs

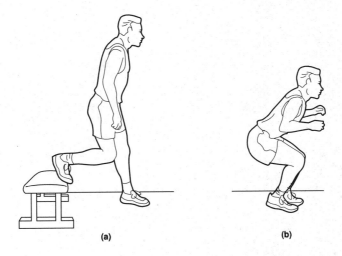

(a) (b)

your ankles, knees, hips, and arms (Figure 11–9b). Try to jump as soon as possible after landing on the ground (i.e., spend as little time on the ground as possible).

3. *Repetition step-down and jump-ups:* Place 2–3 boxes 2–3 feet apart. Jump from the first box to the ground, then up to the next box, then to the ground, and so forth (Figure 11–9c). As your skill and fitness improve, progress from small to larger boxes and jump as quickly as possible between boxes.

Figure 11–9b Step-down, jump-up

Figure 11–9c Repetition step-down and jump-ups

(a) (b) (c) (d)

Variations: Variations are limited only by the imagination. Examples include zigzag box jumping, box jumping followed by cone jumping, one-leg box jumping, and combinations of box and hurdle jumping.

| CAUTION | ◆ | Proceed conservatively with high-impact plyometric exercises. Do not progress to more advanced exercises until you have the necessary fitness and skill. |

High-knee sprint exercise   The high-knee sprint is an excellent exercise for developing sprinting power and fitness for high-intensity exercise. At first, this is physically exhausting and can cause muscle soreness, so progress slowly.

◆   THE TECHNIQUE   Using a sprinting motion, pump your arms vigorously and lift your knees as high and as fast as possible (Figure 11–10). You are almost sprinting in place. Attempt to move only 10 meters (approximately 10 yards) for 20 strides.

Other lower-body speed–power exercises   This chapter has discussed only elementary speed–power exercises. Many other exercises will help you increase power for strength–speed sports. These exercises include the following:

- ◆ *Parachute or harness sprinting:* Various sprint exercises using sprint parachutes (available from sports stores or track and field equipment catalogues), elastic bands, or rope harnesses.
- ◆ *Rope jumping (skipping):* This is the original plyometric exercise. It is great for developing fitness for endurance and high-intensity exercises, as well as leg power.
- ◆ *Downhill sprinting:* Sprinting down a slight incline (e.g., 3 degrees) to overload the large motor units used during sprinting.
- ◆ *Skipping:* This is the same movement you did as a child, except attempt to extend your ankles, knees, and hips fully during the push-off phase of the movement.
- ◆ *Water sprinting:* Sprinting in waist-deep water or in deep water, wearing a life jacket.
- ◆ *Sand sprinting:* Sprinting in loose or hard sand.

Figure 11–10 High-knee sprint exercise

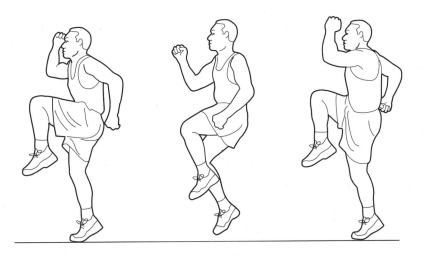

◆ *Olympic weight lifting:* Exercises such as the clean (see Chapter 10), snatch, hang clean or snatch, box clean or snatch, and jerks off the rack are excellent for developing power in most of the major muscle groups of the body. Consult a competent weight-lifting coach for instruction in these lifts.

Basic Upper-Body Power Exercises

There are fewer upper-body plyometric exercises available, probably because most people can't walk on their hands. Medicine balls are excellent for helping you gain upper- and lower-body power.

Bounce push-ups   Do bounce push-up exercises using either the standard or modified push-up position. Begin by doing them against a wall and progressing to the push-up position.

◆   THE TECHNIQUE

- ◆ **Wall bounce push-ups:** Lean against a wall at a 45- to 60-degree angle. Push up forcefully; then allow yourself to go back against the wall and absorb your fall with your arms (Figure 11–11). Immediately push off again.

- ◆ **Bounce push-ups:** From a standard or modified push-up position, push up forcefully, extending your elbows fully until your hands leave the ground. Bounce back to your hands; then repeat the exercise. Begin with 3 to 5 repetitions; then progress gradually.

Variations: "Clap" bounce push-ups (Marine push-ups): Do this exercise as described above, except clap your hands after your hands leave the ground. (That is, push up and leave the ground, clap your hands, bounce back to the push-up position, and repeat.)

Figure 11–11 Bounce push-ups

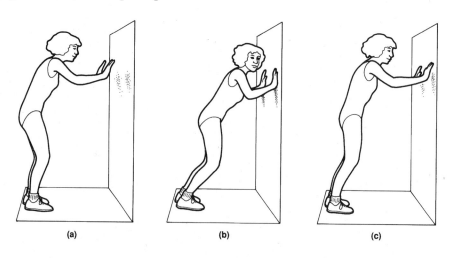

(a)   (b)   (c)

Medicine-ball chest pass   The chest pass is only one of the many exercises you can do with medicine balls.

◆   THE TECHNIQUE   With a partner, stand facing each other, approximately 5 feet apart (Figure 11–12). Hold the ball with both hands at chest level. Pass the ball to your partner by extending your elbows and shoulders (i.e., make a basketball chest pass). Your partner should catch the ball and *immediately* pass the ball back to you, using the same technique. Begin with a light medicine ball; gradually progress to heavy ones.

   Variations: Other exercises include two-arm overhand throw (throwing the medicine ball forcefully overhead), two-arm underhand throw, and one-arm throws.

   Variation: If you don't have a partner, toss the ball into the air using two hands, catch it, then toss it into the air again as quickly as possible. Make sure to bend your knees slightly while doing this exercise.

PEAK-POWER WEIGHT TRAINING

Your **peak power** (weight lifted per second) in most weight-training exercises occurs at approximately 50 percent of the weight you can lift for 1 repetition (1-RM). Training at 50 to 60 percent of 1-RM for approximately 5 repetitions at high speeds is an excellent way to develop power. This technique works best and safest for exercises such as the bench press, where the spine is stabilized and protected.

◆   THE TECHNIQUE   *Peak-power bench press:* Select a weight that's approximately 50 to 60 percent of what you can lift for 1 repetition. With a stopwatch, have a spotter time how long it takes you to complete 5 repetitions. Start the watch as soon as you move the weight downward during the first rep. Stop the watch when you complete the repetitions. Your goal is to complete the repetitions as rapidly as possible. As a rule of thumb, use a weight that's light enough to allow you to complete 5 reps in 7 seconds or less. *Don't bounce the weight against your chest.*

Figure 11–12 Medicine-ball chest pass

COMBINING WEIGHT-TRAINING AND POWER EXERCISES

A new technique for developing muscle power is combining weight-training exercises, such as squats and bench presses, with power exercises, such as jump squats, bounce push-ups, and sprint starts. As examples, do 1 set of 5 repetitions of the squat, then immediately do 5 jump squats. Alternatively, do a set of squats, then do a 30-meter sprint. For the upper body, do a set of bench presses followed immediately by a set of bounce push-ups or medicine-ball tosses with a partner.

Strength–power combination exercises can be specific to your sport. For volleyball players, do a set of squats followed by 5 spiking drills. For shot-putters, do some squats, then put the shot several times. The rationale behind this technique is that the exercises maximize the load on the muscle and nervous systems. Although the technique has not been validated scientifically, it has become very popular with coaches in many sports.

SPEED–POWER TRAINING PROGRAM

Because speed–power training is intense and presents a high risk of injury, it must be done gradually and conservatively. People respond differently to the stress of the program; some people can train almost every day and not feel overly tired or get injured. Others find the workouts extremely stressful. Take it slowly and you probably won't have any problems. Table 11–1 is an example of a beginning speed–power workout.

TABLE 11–1
Beginning Speed–Power Exercise Program

Begin with 1 set of each exercise and progress slowly until you can complete the entire program. Practice this program 2 or 3 days per week. This program is most effective for developing power for sports if combined with a weight-training program and skill practice.

EXERCISE	SETS	VOLUME (REPETITIONS OR OTHER)
Ankle bounce	1–3 sets	10 reps
Squat jumps	1–3 sets	10 reps
Ice skater	1–3 sets	10 reps
Repetitive leaps	1–3 sets	5 reps
High-knee sprint	1–3 sets	10 meters; complete 20 strides
Rope skipping	1–3 sets	1 minute
Bounce push-ups	1–3 sets	10 reps
Medicine-ball chest pass	1–3 sets	10 reps

The ideal speed–power training program includes weight training, speed–power training, and sports practice. Don't overtrain. An example of a balanced program is to train with weights 3 days a week, practice speed–power exercises 2 days a week, and practice your sport 4 or 5 times per week. During the off-season (when you are not actively playing the sport), emphasize weight training and speed–power training. The off-season is an excellent time to develop "base" strength. As the active season begins, cut back on the weight training and emphasize skill development and speed–power training.

YOU CAN DEVELOP MORE SPEED AND POWER!

Until recently, many athletes and coaches thought you had to be born with speed and power. It seemed almost impossible to gain any through training alone. However, although genetics are very important, you *can* learn to sprint faster and jump higher. Start with these beginning exercises and you will be amazed at how much you can improve in 2 to 3 months of training.

C H A P T E R

12 Nutrition for Weight Training

NUTRITION PLAYS AN IMPORTANT ROLE IN DETERMINING THE EFFECTIVENESS OF A FITNESS and weight-control program. Keeping off excess body fat is difficult through exercise alone. Weight training helps build muscle but is not a good way to burn off many calories. Unless you combine it with good nutrition and endurance exercise, you probably are doomed to failure in fighting the "battle of the bulge."

We are bombarded with nutritional information—some of it helpful but too much of it junk. Beware of nutritional advice that seems too good to be true. There are no nutritional supplements or drugs that will turn a weak, flabby individual into a strong, healthy person. Major changes call for hard work and dedication. Instant "cures," such as megavitamin therapy or "fat-burning" pills, don't work and are either dangerous or expensive. You are better off staying with the proven principles of nutrition and participating in a steady, progressive fitness program.

Nutrition is also important for exercise performance. Scientists are beginning to appreciate the role of diet and nutritional manipulation in athletic success. Although the **balanced diet** is still the cornerstone of the well-rounded fitness program, various dietary techniques also have been effective in improving performance.

PLANNING A HEALTHY DIET

In 1992 (updated in 1996) the U.S. Department of Agriculture (USDA), advised by nutritional scientists, developed guidelines for proper nutrition, termed the "Food Guide Pyramid" (Figure 12–1). Eat more foods from the base of the pyramid and fewer from the top.

Figure 12–1 The Food Guide Pyramid recommended by the USDA has, as its basis, the consumption of bread, cereals, pasta, fruits, and vegetables. Milk and protein foods have lower priority, and fats and sweets are to be consumed only sparingly. *Source:* Food Guide Pyramid, Consumer Information Center, USDA, Pueblo, CO.

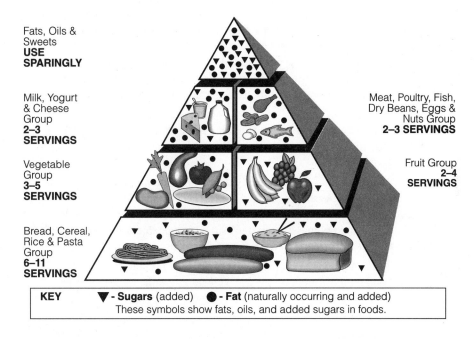

Fats, Oils &
Sweets
**USE
SPARINGLY**

Milk, Yogurt
& Cheese
Group
**2–3
SERVINGS**

Meat, Poultry, Fish,
Dry Beans, Eggs &
Nuts Group
2–3 SERVINGS

Vegetable
Group
**3–5
SERVINGS**

Fruit Group
**2–4
SERVINGS**

Bread, Cereal,
Rice & Pasta
Group
**6–11
SERVINGS**

KEY   ▼ **- Sugars** (added)   ● **- Fat** (naturally occurring and added)
These symbols show fats, oils, and added sugars in foods.

Complex carbohydrate foods, such as bread, cereal, rice, and pasta, form the base of the pyramid. The largest proportion of foods in your diet should come from this group (6–11 servings). These foods supply thiamin, iron, niacin, and fiber and are critical for satisfying the energy requirements of a vigorous exercise program.

Fruits and vegetables form the next, smaller layer of the pyramid. Every day, eat 3–5 servings from the vegetable group and 2–4 servings from the fruit group. These foods are important for supplying vitamins, minerals, and fiber. It is particularly important to eat dark-green and deep-yellow vegetables because of their high nutrient content and their possible influence in reducing the risk of certain types of cancer.

The next layer of the pyramid contains dairy products (2–3 servings per day) and high-protein foods, such as meats, poultry, fish, beans, nuts, and eggs (2–3 servings). These foods supply iron, thiamin, riboflavin, niacin, phosphorus, and zinc in addition to protein. Avoid eating meats with a high fat content because they are associated with increased risk of coronary artery disease. In women, this is particularly important after menopause, when the coronary artery disease risk is about the same as in men.

At the top of the pyramid are fats, oils, and sweets. These should be consumed only in small quantities.

The USDA guidelines stress the following:

1. *Eat a variety of foods.* Vary the foods you eat so that you obtain the nutrients you need for good health. Use the Food Guide Pyramid to help you choose the appropriate number of servings for each food group.

2. *Balance the food you eat with physical activity: maintain or improve your weight.* Follow the U.S. Surgeon General's recommendation on exercise and health, and every day get at least 30 minutes of some type of physical activity. Preferably, follow a structured exercise program. When attempting to lose weight, do so gradually. Choose low-fat, low-calorie, nutrient-dense foods, rather than fatty foods, sugar and sweets, and alcoholic beverages.

3. *Choose a diet with plenty of grain products, vegetables, and fruits.* These foods provide nutrients, energy, and fiber and are low in fats. Eat a variety of these foods.

4. *Choose a diet low in fat, saturated fat, and cholesterol.* High-fat diets increase the risk of coronary artery diesease, cancer, and obesity. Limit fat intake to 30 percent or less of your total calorie intake, and stress monounsaturated and polyunsaturated fats, such as vegetable oils, nuts, and fish, over saturated fats found in deep-fried fast foods.

5. *Choose a diet moderate in sugars.* High-sugar foods tend to be low in nutrients and promote tooth decay. Carbohydrates are the most important fuel for intense exercise. Stress fruits and grains over baked goods, candies, and presweetened breakfast cereals.

6. *Choose a diet moderate in salt and sodium.* Too much salt and sodium promotes high blood pressure in some people and may promote calcium loss, contributing to osteoporosis (bone loss). Check food labels and avoid foods that contain a lot of salt, such as salted snack foods and luncheon meats.

7. *If you drink alcoholic beverages, do so in moderation.* Moderate drinking, which may reduce the risk of cardiovascular disease, is no more than one drink per day for women and two drinks per day for men. Higher levels of alcohol consumption are associated with a higher risk of many diseases and premature death from unintentional injuries.

Fluids are a particularly important part of an active person's diet because they directly affect exercise capacity. Body water is an important component in most of the body's biochemical reactions and helps maintain blood volume and control body temperature. Many people avoid drinking water or other fluids because they are afraid of gaining "water weight." However, fluids are critical for health and performance. Worry about body fat instead of body weight.

A variety of effective fluid replacements have been developed for active people that not only satisfy the body's fluid requirements but also provide energy during exercise and hasten recovery after a vigorous workout. (These products are discussed later in this chapter.)

Vitamins

Incredible amounts of money are spent on **vitamin** and mineral pills every year, by both athletes and nonathletes. In the United States, however, the only common documented deficiencies are iron and calcium. Therefore, with a couple of possible exceptions, anything more than a balanced diet and maybe a "one-a-day" vitamin/mineral pill is useless and a waste of money.

Vitamins act as coenzymes (work with enzymes to drive the body's metabolism) and aid in the production and protection of red blood cells. Vitamins are not produced in the body and must be consumed in the diet, but they are needed in only extremely small amounts. Exercise may increase requirements for vitamin C, thiamin, pyridoxine, and riboflavin. Only vitamins C, E, pantothenic acid, and thiamin have been shown to have any effects on exercise performance. Many positive studies using these vitamins have used animal or vitamin-deficient human subjects.

Vitamin C supplementation has been a fertile area of debate since Linus Pauling suggested that megadoses of the vitamin can cure and prevent the common cold. His contention has been extremely controversial, and only a few medical studies have supported his claims. It is certain that debate on this issue will continue for many years. Several studies suggest that Vitamin E supplementation may prevent coronary artery disease.

However, it appears that vitamin supplements improve performance only if there is a nutritional deficiency. To be on the safe side, you might consider taking a basic vitamin supplement. There is apparently no justification for the megadoses of vitamins taken by many athletes, though. Moreover, high doses of vitamins have been shown to cause toxic side effects in some people. The best advice is to eat a balanced diet from the basic six food groups.

Iron

Iron intake in active women is often inadequate. As many as 25 to 80 percent of women endurance athletes could be iron-deficient. A great deal of iron is lost through the feces, urine, sweat, and menstrual blood.

Menstruating women need about 18 mg of iron a day but typically take in only 12 mg per day. This can lead to a drop in iron stores in the bone marrow and, eventually, to iron-deficiency anemia (low blood count). Bone marrow is found inside many bones and is the site for red blood cell production. Iron deficiency, even without anemia, leads to impaired performance and fatigue.

Iron found in meat, fish, and chicken is absorbed by the body much more easily than iron in other foods. It is recommended, therefore, that active women eat meat, fish, or chicken or take an iron supplement every day. Some people, however, cannot tolerate iron supplements. Check with your doctor for advice about your iron needs. A simple test that measures blood ferritin can tell your doctor if you are iron-deficient.

A recent study in Finland has shown a link between high iron levels in men and coronary artery disease. The practical significance of this finding is not known, and further research is necessary before specific dietary advice is available.

To sum up, iron supplements are beneficial if you are iron-deficient. Iron has a marked effect on the body's endurance capacity and the ability to transport oxygen.

Calcium

Osteoporosis, or weakening of the bones, is a common problem in postmenopausal women and in some men over 50 years of age. Three factors that affect bone weakening in women are estrogen (a female hormone), calcium in the diet, and exercise. Until recently, this condition was of little interest to younger women. However, it has been found that active women who have irregular menstrual cycles sometimes have decreased bone density. (In general, active women have denser bones than inactive women.)

Decreased bone density in active young women is thought to be due to low levels of estrogen. Heavy exercise training can depress estrogen production. Calcium in the diet may also be an important factor. Women with normal estrogen levels should take in at least 1000 mg of dietary calcium per day. Those with low estrogen levels do not absorb calcium as well, so they need at least 1500 mg per day. Dairy products — such as milk, yogurt, cottage cheese, ice cream, and hard cheese — are excellent sources of calcium. Another good source is soft-boned fish, such as salmon, trout, and sardines.

Take a calcium supplement if you can't get enough in your diet. The best calcium supplements are calcium carbonate or calcium phosphate because they are most readily absorbed. Beware of calcium supplements containing bone meal and dolomite — they often contain high levels of lead, mercury, and arsenic.

The Energy Requirements of Active People

Most body functions, including muscle contractions that allow us to lift weights and do other physical tasks, are made possible by the energy supplied by foods. Carbohydrates, fats, and proteins are the three basic food components. All are essential for supplying the body's energy needs.

Active people must take in enough calories to satisfy the energy requirements of physical activity and provide the nutrients necessary for good health. Again, this can be done by consuming a well-balanced diet containing enough calories to satisfy the body's needs but not so many that you become overweight.

DEVELOPING AN ATTRACTIVE BODY: THE ROLE OF EXERCISE AND NUTRITION

The main reason for the tremendous popularity of weight training is that it improves physical appearance. People who train with weights often look more athletic, tighter, and more muscular than other people. Paradoxically, some people use weight training to help them gain weight whereas others use it to lose weight. Is this possible? Yes, if you understand the principle of energy balance as it applies to body composition.

Weight Training, Energy Balance, and Body Composition

All the energy absorbed by the body in the form of food must be accounted for — as energy used for body functions, energy stored as fat, or energy wasted, in the form of heat. There is no other place for food energy to go. If less energy is taken in than needed, fat is lost.

It is difficult to significantly affect energy balance through weight training because it calls for few calories (compared to activities such as long-distance running). However, weight training can affect energy balance indirectly. Lifting weight increases muscle mass, one of the most metabolically active tissues in the body. People who go on low-calorie diets to lose weight usually lose a lot of muscle mass. Consequently, their metabolic rate decreases and lost fat is regained easily. Weight training spares muscle mass and helps maintain metabolic rate so that weight-loss programs are more successful.

Contrary to popular belief, you cannot **spot reduce** — you cannot reduce fat in a particular area through exercise. Studies have shown that spot reducing doesn't happen from exercise. However, weight training can have an enormous effect on physical appearance, even if body fat is unaltered.

Strengthening a body part, such as the abdominal muscles, increases muscle tone and "tightens up" the area. Strong abdominal muscles are less likely to sag, so the area looks more attractive. Excess fat stays — but it looks better. Weight training can play a role in helping people gain or lose weight, or simply look more attractive, if it is practiced as part of a comprehensive diet and exercise program.

Losing Weight

Weight loss is a national obsession. Many people train with weights or do other exercises to control their weight. Ultimately, the body's energy balance determines whether body fat increases, decreases, or stays the same. Fat increases when more energy is consumed than expended. Although exercise is an important part of a weight-control program, caloric restriction is essential if the program is to be successful.

The goal of a weight-control program should be to lose body fat and maintain the loss. Quick-loss programs often lead to loss of muscle tissue and body water. They do nothing to instill healthy long-term dietary habits that will maintain the new weight. The following principles for losing body fat will increase the chances of success for a weight-control program:

- Stress fat loss. Rapid weight loss from fad diets is often caused by the loss of muscle mass and body water. Fat loss instead of weight loss should be the goal.

- Restrict the weight you lose. Lose no more than 1½ or 2 pounds per week. More rapid weight loss results in loss of muscle tissue and body water.

- Eat a balanced diet high in complex carbohydrates and low in fat. Lose calories by combining caloric restriction with more exercise.

- Exercise, particularly endurance exercise, is critically important for a successful weight-loss program. The best exercises for losing weight include running, walking, and cycling. Weight training helps maintain muscle mass during weight loss.

- Monitor your body composition. Make sure that most of the weight loss is from a reduction in body fat instead of a reduction in **fat-free weight.**

Gaining Weight

Many people are naturally underweight and seek to gain weight. There are two basic ways to increase body weight: increasing muscle or increasing fat. Lean people can often increase body fat with little or no adverse effect on appearance or health; nevertheless, they should strive to gain "quality weight." This can be done only through a vigorous weight-training program that stresses the large-muscle groups in the legs, hips, shoulders, arms, and chest.

Muscle weight takes many years to gain but is surely preferable to the fat that is quickly added from expensive high-calorie weight gain supplements or unhealthy high-fat diets. These are basic guidelines for gaining weight:

- ◆ Stress quality over quantity (increase muscle rather than fat). Carrying extra fat does little to improve your physical performance or appearance.

- ◆ Use weight training to increase the size of major muscle groups. Emphasize exercises that work large-muscle groups: mainly presses (e.g., bench press, seated press) and high-resistance leg exercises (e.g., squats, leg presses). For lifts, use heavy resistance and many sets (e.g., 5 sets of 5 repetitions).

- ◆ Concentrate on long-term gains. Do not expect to increase fat-free weight by more than 4 to 6 pounds per year.

- ◆ Don't use drugs to gain weight. Avoid anabolic steroids and growth hormone. Anabolic steroids increase the risk of coronary artery and liver disease and have many serious side effects. Growth hormone can cause permanent disfigurement and can permanently impair insulin metabolism. The benefits are not worth the risks.

- ◆ Eat a well-balanced diet containing slightly more calories than normal. If you are training vigorously, your protein requirement may increase slightly to 1–1.5 grams per kilogram body weight.

- ◆ Monitor your body composition. Keep track of your progress by measuring your fat-free weight and body fat. The underwater weighing technique is the most accurate. This test is done in many college and university physical education departments, sports-medicine centers, and health clubs. The skinfold and electrical impedance techniques of body-composition measurement are also widely available. Ask your instructor for further information.

- ◆ Consult a physician if you do not progress. There are a variety of explanations for being chronically underweight, including family history, maturational level, smoking, or metabolic status.

Weight control is important for health, appearance, and athletic performance. However, excessive preoccupation with weight control and food can lead to eating disorders.

EATING DISORDERS

Being thin and young is presented by the media as ideal for women. This has resulted in an epidemic of eating disorders in industrialized countries. Over 90 percent of all people with anorexia nervosa and bulimia are women.

Men are not immune from such compulsive behavior, but they display it differently than women. Men who exercise to excess, even when severely injured, are called obligatory runners.

These men run more than 50 miles a week. When they can't exercise, they become extremely depressed. The common denominator in these conditions in men and women is not known.

Anorexia Nervosa and Anorexia Athletica

These eating disorders are closely related. **Anorexia nervosa** is an obsessive preoccupation with food and fear of weight. The person uses extreme diets and becomes focused on becoming thin at the expense of other goals. **Anorexia athletica** is a variation of anorexia nervosa in which, besides severe dieting, the person overdoes exercise.

Typically, the person with anorexia is a young woman of high school or college age. She is seen by parents and friends as being extremely conscientious, with an overly organized life. She usually has low self-esteem and an extreme wish to please others. She may have a slight weight problem. However, these are only generalizations. Sometimes, anorexia may develop because of depression, illness, or peer pressure.

Women often report experiencing a type of "high" when they first use their punishing diet routine. Researchers have speculated that this may be a result of the increased attention they get from losing weight. It has also been suggested that the "high" comes from the body's releasing of hormones called endorphins to combat the intense feelings of hunger accompanying the diet. Endorphins produce an effect similar to opium and are one of the body's ways of dealing with pain.

As the condition develops, the person will use a stricter diet and do more exercise. Physical signs common to individuals with anorexia include extreme weight loss, dry skin, hair loss, brittle fingernails, cold hands and feet, low blood pressure and heart rate, swelling around the ankles and hands, and weakening of the bones. Anorexia nervosa is characterized by the following:

- *Extreme weight loss.* A woman with anorexia typically loses at least 25 percent of her original weight. With the weight loss, she often experiences insomnia (inability to sleep) and a decreased ability to tolerate cold. She may wear many layers of clothes to keep her warm and hide her extreme weight loss.

- *Unrealistic body image.* She sees herself as overweight, even when others describe her as painfully thin. This image becomes more distorted as she loses weight.

- *Extreme diets.* She restricts food intake for extended periods, even when extremely hungry. She usually will try to eliminate carbohydrates from the diet and often becomes a vegetarian.

- *Obsession with food.* She will often daydream about food, able to think of nothing else. She may prepare elaborate meals for others as part of her obsession with food. She also has a great fear of losing control and gaining back all the weight she has lost. She lives by the notion that she can't lose enough weight and still has a long way to go.

- *Drug use.* She may abuse drugs, particularly stimulants such as amphetamines, which depress appetite. She may use emetics to help her vomit, diuretics to lose water weight, and laxatives to clear out the digestive tract. (The excessive use of laxatives leads to constipation in people with anorexia.)

- *Amenorrhea.* It is likely she will stop menstruating. This happens early in the condition, even before much weight is lost.

- *Excessive exercise.* She uses exercise as a way of losing more weight. She often runs herself to exhaustion and extreme weakness.

- *Depression.* The woman with anorexia probably feels extremely depressed. She has very low self-esteem, decreased sex drive, feelings of hopelessness, and sometimes suicidal thoughts.

Bulimia

A person with **bulimia** will go on an eating binge and consume thousands of calories. Usually, but not always, the person induces vomiting after the binge. People with bulimia are often also anorexic, but not necessarily. After the eating binge, the person is typically very depressed and ashamed and usually resolves to go on a stricter diet. This leads to a vicious cycle of binge eating and dieting.

People with longstanding bulimia usually are dehydrated and have decayed teeth, enlarged salivary glands, abnormally low levels of potassium and chloride in the blood, and abnormal heart rhythms and brain waves.

Treating Eating Disorders

Because eating disorders are so common, you should be aware of their warning signs and risk factors. The physical signs—excessive weight loss, low blood pressure, obsessive behavior, dry skin, cold hands and feet—have been discussed. Young women who are slightly overweight and have low self-esteem are at greatest risk. The best thing you can do is recognize you have the problem early. Treatments are not very effective for people who have had these eating disorders for a long time.

Treatment should fit the severity of the problem. You could have one or two physical symptoms typical of anorexia without actually having the condition. Perhaps you just need to learn about good eating habits. You should get a checkup, too. If there is any possibility that you or one of your friends has an eating disorder, however, seek psychological counseling and medical help right away.

Medical treatment includes hospitalization to stabilize serious cases, medications to treat depression, and behavior modification to change eating habits. Anorexia and bulimia can cause serious health problems and even death. They should not be taken lightly.

Certain social and psychological factors increase the risk of developing these disorders:

- The belief that the only way to be beautiful and happy is to be thin

- Family history of eating disorders

- Lack of emotional support from one's family

- Overemphasis on achievement

- Rigid, overprotective parents

If you have any risk factors or overt symptoms of eating disorders, seek help from your physician or counselor before you have a serious problem on your hands. You don't have to commit to long-term treatment. A meeting may help you understand if you do have an eating disorder or are just undergoing the normal, temporary setbacks of living.

DIET AND PERFORMANCE

Carbohydrates are the essential fuel for muscular work. They are stored in your muscles and liver as **glycogen.** Although fats and proteins are used for energy during exercise, carbohydrates' contribution to supplying energy increases with the intensity of physical activity. When your body or individual muscles are depleted of glycogen, fatigue and sluggishness set in, limiting performance.

The amount of glycogen present in the liver and muscles when exercise begins will affect endurance, capacity for intense exercise, and even mental outlook. If your muscles feel tired, you are unlikely to have an effective workout or successful competition. Glycogen depletion causes fatigue, and if normal glycogen levels are not restored, performance levels will be impaired. The goal of an optimal athletic nutrition program is to prevent glycogen depletion during exercise and to replenish glycogen stores in the muscles and the liver immediately after exercise. These goals can be accomplished by eating a high-energy, high-carbohydrate diet during periods of intense training or competition and consuming carbohydrate beverages during and after training.

Preventing Glycogen Depletion

Glycogen depletion may be avoided to a certain extent by using fats as fuels during exercise. This spares the muscle and liver glycogen stores. There are several ways to do this: (1) improve your ability to use fats, (2) mobilize fats early during exercise, and (3) provide alternative fuels for the muscles to slow down the use of glycogen and blood sugar.

The best way to improve your ability to use fats is through endurance training. Endurance training increases the size of structures called mitochondria, which are the energy centers of the cells. This facilitates fat utilization.

The sooner you can make alternative fuels available, the sooner you can use them, sparing important carbohydrate stores. Another technique used to increase fat mobilization is ingesting caffeine. The use of carbohydrate drinks during exercise has also been shown to be effective in sparing muscle and liver glycogen and maintaining blood sugar. Although caffeine ingestion before exercise and drinking carbohydrate beverages during exercise have proven effective in endurance exercise, their effects on strength exercises are not completely understood. Caffeine, found in such foods as coffee, chocolate, and tea, causes nervousness and stomach upset in some people, so it cannot be universally recommended as a means of sparing glycogen stores.

The High-Carbohydrate Diet

A high-carbohydrate diet is critical for athletes involved in heavy training. It contains the basic six food groups but stresses food from the carbohydrate groups, such as cereals, fruits, and grains.

Figure 12–2 Effect of diet on performance

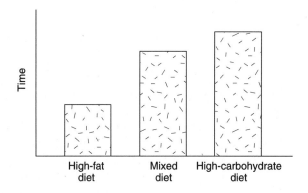

Many studies have shown that this diet enables active people to exercise longer and more intensely and recover faster than those on mixed or high-fat diets (Figure 12–2). Table 12–1 gives an example of a high-energy, high-carbohydrate diet that is suitable for any active person involved in intense training. This diet includes fresh vegetables for vitamins and minerals and meats and meat substitutes for protein, and it avoids refined sugar products, such as cakes, pies, and candies. Drinking alcoholic beverages should also be avoided or minimized.

Most people do not train hard enough to fully benefit from a high-carbohydrate diet, but active people should take great care in designing their diets. It is important that enough calories and protein be consumed to optimize muscle growth. Too much carbohydrate in the diet will lead to fat gain. There is no one perfect diet. Experiment with a variety of foods to find a diet that's agreeable and palatable.

Carbohydrate Drinks During Exercise

A recent finding in sports-medicine research has been the discovery that consuming carbohydrate drinks during exercise improves performance. These drinks enhance glycogen stores in the liver, maintain blood-sugar levels during exercise, and decrease the rate of glycogen breakdown in muscles — all of which improve exercise performance.

Just as important, the use of carbohydrate drinks immediately after exercise results in a rapid resynthesis of glycogen. Researchers have found that the 2-hour period immediately after exercise is the best time for restoring glycogen in the muscles and liver. If you consume carbohydrate drinks during this time, you can increase glycogen levels by 20 percent.

Specially formulated athletic fluid-replacement drinks containing carbohydrates are excellent for maintaining blood sugar and replacing lost glycogen. Drinking a carbohydrate beverage during and immediately after exercise allows you to come back sooner after a hard workout and possibly prevent the feeling of fatigue accompanying low glycogen levels.

Avoid High-Fat Diets

In years past, a breakfast of bacon, eggs, and toast smothered in butter was almost a tradition in the United States. Today many people avoid such meals because of their high fat and

---

TABLE 12–1

Example of a Diet High in Energy and Carbohydrates

BREAKFAST

1 cup fruit juice (orange, grapefruit, guava)
Pancakes (2–3) with syrup
2 eggs (cholesterol-free egg substitutes)
Turkey sausage
Nonfat milk or hot chocolate

LUNCH

Tuna salad sandwich
Fruit
Green salad
Nonfat milk

DINNER

Pasta with meat sauce (spaghetti, lasagna, etc.)
Bread
Green salad
Fruit
Nonfat milk

---

cholesterol content. Studies show that diets high in fat and cholesterol increase the risk of **coronary artery disease** (hardening of the arteries) and some types of cancer.

Both the American Heart Association and the American Cancer Society recommend diets low in fat and cholesterol. So the high-carbohydrate diet that has been recommended not only will improve your physical performance but may improve your health as well.

Protein Requirements for Weight Trainers

Protein supplements have been popular among weight trainers for many years. However, most people who train with weights don't need any more protein than the average person. The daily requirement for protein in healthy adults is about 0.8–1.0 gram of protein per kilogram of body weight. However, several recent studies suggest that athletes involved in extremely intense programs may have a higher protein requirement than average.

Protein requirements are determined by a complicated and difficult procedure called nitrogen balance. Proteins are composed of different combinations of **amino acids.** Amino acids contain nitrogen, and the nitrogen must be eliminated to use the amino acids as fuel. Nitrogen is an important marker of protein metabolism because its elimination from the body is directly proportional to the breakdown of amino acids.

Protein breakdown in the body can be estimated by measuring nitrogen loss from the body in waste products such as urine, feces, sweat, nail clippings, hair loss, and so on. Protein intake can be estimated by measuring the quantity of nitrogen ingested in the diet. If the body is using more protein for fuel than is being taken in (a net loss of nitrogen), the person is said to be in "negative nitrogen balance." If the person is incorporating more protein into body tissues than is being expended as fuel (a net gain in nitrogen), then the body is said to be in "positive nitrogen balance."

The goal for people involved in a weight-training program is to achieve a positive nitrogen balance (or at least to prevent a negative nitrogen balance). Positive nitrogen balance means that the body is adding protein and suggests that muscles are getting bigger and stronger. Factors important in muscle growth include muscle tension from weight training, adequate protein and calories in the diet, and sufficient rest between workouts.

Nitrogen-balance studies usually show that most active people do not need more protein in their diet. The average requirement of 0.8–1.0 gram of protein per kilogram of body weight is easily satisfied by the average American diet. Extra protein probably is necessary only for elite or experienced weight-trained athletes involved in very intense training. However, the need for added protein in active people is actively debated by scientists. Surely, for people training at less intense levels, protein supplements are unnecessary.

Proteins as an Energy Source

Most energy during exercise comes from carbohydrates and fats. However, proteins are used for energy, and they help maintain blood sugar through a process called gluconeogenesis (the formation of new blood sugar in the liver). Maintenance of blood sugar during exercise is critical for sustaining exercise intensity. Low blood sugar causes fatigue, sluggishness, and disorientation.

Because of its effects on blood sugar and metabolic regulation, the pregame or preexercise meal should contain some protein. For many years, physicians treating people with diabetes mellitus, a disease related to faulty blood-sugar regulation, have recommended a diet with a significant protein component because the amino acids are very effective in ensuring long-lasting release of sugar into the blood. In essence, the amino acids act like tiny blood-glucose-releasing capsules.

Amino Acid and Polypeptide Supplements

Amino acid and polypeptide supplements have been hailed as "natural" anabolic steroids that accelerate muscle development, decrease body fat, and stimulate the release of growth hormone. Amino acids are the basic building blocks of proteins, and polypeptides are combinations of two or more amino acids linked together. Proponents of amino acid and polypeptide supplements point to their more rapid absorption as proof of superiority to normal dietary sources of protein.

Presently, there is little scientific proof to support the need for amino acid or polypeptide supplementation in most active people. The protein requirement of most people who train with weights is no higher than for sedentary individuals. So the rate of amino acid absorption from the gastrointestinal tract is not important. For recreational weight trainers, these supplements are a waste of money.

Some indirect proof exists, however, that amino acid or polypeptide supplements may be beneficial in elite weight-trained athletes. Muscle hypertrophy (enlargement) depends on the concentration of amino acids in the muscle — the more amino acids available, the faster the rate of muscle hypertrophy. Several studies have shown that elite weight-trained athletes often do not consume enough protein. Also, when very large amounts of protein were consumed, muscle hypertrophy was accelerated. This issue is controversial among exercise physiology researchers.

These supplements do involve risks. Consuming an unbalanced amino acid formula, one that is high in some amino acids and deficient in others, may cause negative nitrogen balance. Also, substituting amino acid or polypeptide supplements for protein-rich foods may cause deficiencies in important nutrients such as iron and the B vitamins. Clearly, amino acid supplementation is of little use to the average recreational weight trainer. So, unless you are an elite athlete, just stick to the well-balanced diet.

Other Nutritional Supplements

As discussed, it is difficult to improve on the balanced diet. However, various nutritional supplements have been studied as possible **ergogenic aids** — substances or techniques that improve performance (Table 12–2). Possible nutritional ergogenic aids that have been studied recently include creatine monohydrate, phosphatidylserine, medium-chain triglycerides, L-carnitine, succinates, and pyridoxine-alpha-ketoglutarate. Studies of these substances have yielded contradictory results. Some studies show that all of these substances can improve performance; other studies show no effect. At this point, therefore, it is not appropriate to recommend these supplements.

ANABOLIC STEROIDS

Anabolic steroids are drugs that resemble the male hormone **testosterone.** Athletes consume them in the hope of gaining weight, strength, power, speed, endurance, and aggressiveness. They work by speeding up protein synthesis in target tissue and, possibly, by preventing protein breakdown. The drugs are widely used by athletes involved in track and field, weight lifting, and American football. A particularly disturbing trend is anabolic steroid use by nonathletic high school students hoping to improve appearance and sex appeal.

Many people who take these drugs are unaware of the risks involved. People usually take anabolic steroids without medical supervision. Many reports in the medical literature relate serious illness and even death in athletes who took anabolic steroids. Legally, anabolic steroids are available by prescription; physicians, however, are forbidden from prescribing these drugs to improve athletic performance. Anabolic steroids are now classified as controlled substances. Illegal possession of them carries the same penalties as do other illegal drugs, such as cocaine.

Scores of studies and articles have described the effects of these drugs on patients and athletes. Unfortunately, the research findings have been extremely inconsistent, some studies showing substantial gains in performance and others showing no effect. After summarizing published studies on the effects of anabolic steroids on athletic performance and health, the American College of Sports Medicine issued a position statement on anabolic steroid use. It stated that although anabolic steroids probably improve athletic performance, benefits are probably small and not worth the health risks involved.

TABLE 12–2

Some Techniques and Substances Used as Ergogenic Aids

Alcohol
Amphetamines
Anabolic steroids
Aspartates
Bee pollen
Beta blockers
Caffeine
Cocaine
Cold
Creatine monohydrate
Digitalis
Electrical stimulation
Ephedrine
Epinephrine
Glucose
Growth hormone
Heat
Human chorionic gonadotropin
Hypnosis
Inosine
Insulin
Lactate
Marijuana
Massage
Medium-chain triglycerides
Negatively ionized air
Nicotine
Nitroglycerine
Norepinephrine
Oxygen
Phosphatidylserine
Protein supplements
Pyridoxine-alpha-ketoglutarate
Sodium bicarbonate
Strychnine
Succinates
Sulfa drugs
Vitamins
Wheat germ oil
Yeast

Two very popular supplements with weight trainers are **dehydroepiandrosterone** (DHEA) and **androstenedione** (Andro). These hormones are produced by your adrenal glands and are widely available in health-food stores and many other retail outlets. They are broken down quickly into testosterone and, to a certain extent, estrogen. For this reason, their effects are similar to those of anabolic steroids. Potentially, they can also have many of the same side effects. Little is known of their effectiveness or risks. They are not recommended.

Anabolic Steroids and Health

Although anabolic steroids may increase muscle size and strength in some people, they are potentially dangerous substances that can have severe side effects (see Table 12−3). Most athletes do not experience serious short-term side effects, provided the dosage is moderate. However, long-term use has led to severe effects, including death. The long-term consequences of anabolic steroid use in healthy athletes are not completely understood. Anabolic steroid use may result in coronary artery disease and liver cancer, but these conditions may take many years to develop. Anabolic steroid use has been linked with severe psychiatric disorders. Some experts think the drugs are addictive. Anabolic steroids also impair the immune system, making it more difficult for the body to fight off disease. Some anabolic steroids are injected. Sharing needles increases the risk of acquired immune deficiency syndrome (AIDS).

TABLE 12–3
Reported Side Effects of Anabolic Steroids

Abnormal bleeding and blood clotting
Acne
Breast enlargement in males
Decreased male-hormone levels
Depressed sperm production
Dizziness
Elevated blood pressure
Elevated blood sugar
Gastrointestinal distress
Coronary artery disease
Impaired immune function
Increased aggressiveness
Liver cancer
Liver toxicity
Masculinization in women and children
Prostate cancer
Stunted growth in children
Tissue swelling

A person who doesn't experience any side effects from the drugs early on may be setting the stage for serious disease in later life. In general, the severity of steroid side effects seems to be affected by the dosage and duration of drug therapy. Athletes taking anabolic steroids may be taking an unnecessary chance.

Anabolic Steroid Use by Women

Anabolic steroid use by women has been reported in athletes involved in swimming, track and field, and body building. Anabolic steroids have been detected in female athletes during drug tests done during international competitions. The incredible level of muscle development in some female athletes who train with weights (i.e., body builders, swimmers, throwers, and weight lifters) has increased suspicions about drug use in athletes in these sports.

Women can expect greater gains than men from steroid use because they have naturally low levels of male hormones. However, the side effects are more severe. Women who take anabolic steroids often experience masculinization, such as deepening of the voice and facial hair growth. Other side effects include acne, changes in skin texture, severe fluid retention, unnatural increases in muscle mass, and radically changed cholesterol metabolism. Females may also experience clitoral enlargement and menstrual irregularity. Many of these changes are irreversible. The effects on future fertility are unknown.

Anabolic Steroid Use by Children

Children who take anabolic steroids will first experience accelerated maturation followed by premature closure of the growth centers in the long bones. If anabolic steroid use begins early in adolescence, the ultimate height of the person may be less.

A P P E N D I X   1

Muscular System

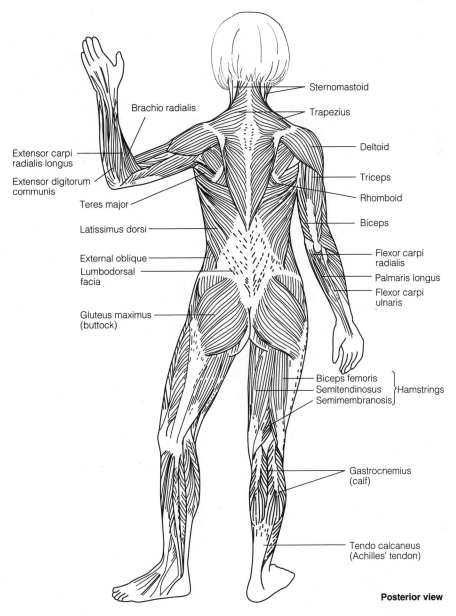

Sternomastoid

Brachio radialis

Trapezius

Deltoid

Extensor carpi
radialis longus

Triceps

Extensor digitorum
communis

Rhomboid

Teres major

Biceps

Latissimus dorsi

Flexor carpi
radialis

External oblique

Palmaris longus

Lumbodorsal
facia

Flexor carpi
ulnaris

Gluteus maximus
(buttock)

Biceps femoris
Semitendinosus   } Hamstrings
Semimembranosis

Gastrocnemius
(calf)

Tendo calcaneus
(Achilles' tendon)

Posterior view

173

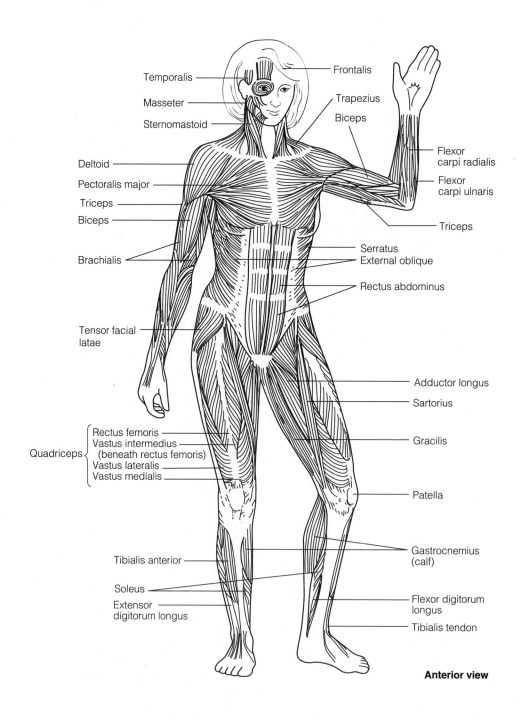

Temporalis

Masseter

Sternomastoid

Deltoid

Pectoralis major

Triceps

Biceps

Brachialis

Tensor facial latae

Quadriceps {
Rectus femoris
Vastus intermedius (beneath rectus femoris)
Vastus lateralis
Vastus medialis
}

Tibialis anterior

Soleus

Extensor digitorum longus

Frontalis

Trapezius

Biceps

Flexor carpi radialis

Flexor carpi ulnaris

Triceps

Serratus

External oblique

Rectus abdominus

Adductor longus

Sartorius

Gracilis

Patella

Gastrocnemius (calf)

Flexor digitorum longus

Tibialis tendon

Anterior view

APPENDIX 2

Free Weight and Machine Exercises for Sports and Activities

WEIGHT TRAINING FOR SPORTS AND ACTIVITIES

Emphasize these body parts when training for the following sports and activities. Although it is important to condition all major muscle groups, specific activities require extra conditioning in specific muscles.

Activity or Sport	Neck	Shoulders	Chest	Arms	Forearms	Upper Back	Lower Back	Abdominals	Thighs	Hamstrings	Calves
Badminton		✔	✔	✔	✔	✔			✔	✔	✔
Basketball		✔	✔			✔	✔	✔	✔	✔	✔
Billiards		✔		✔	✔	✔	✔				
Canoeing		✔	✔	✔	✔	✔	✔	✔			
Cycling		✔		✔	✔	✔	✔	✔	✔	✔	✔
Dancing							✔	✔	✔	✔	✔
Fishing				✔	✔				✔	✔	✔
Field hockey		✔	✔	✔	✔	✔	✔	✔	✔	✔	✔
Football	✔	✔	✔	✔	✔	✔	✔	✔	✔	✔	✔
Golf		✔		✔	✔	✔	✔	✔	✔	✔	✔
Gymnastics		✔	✔	✔	✔	✔	✔	✔	✔	✔	✔
Jogging		✔		✔		✔	✔	✔	✔	✔	✔
Skiing, snow		✔		✔		✔	✔	✔	✔	✔	✔
Skiing, water	✔	✔		✔	✔	✔	✔	✔	✔	✔	✔
Scuba diving				✔		✔	✔	✔	✔	✔	
Squash		✔	✔	✔	✔	✔	✔	✔	✔	✔	✔
Swimming		✔	✔	✔	✔	✔	✔	✔	✔	✔	
Table tennis		✔		✔	✔	✔			✔	✔	✔
Tennis		✔	✔	✔	✔	✔	✔	✔	✔	✔	✔
Volleyball		✔	✔	✔	✔	✔	✔	✔	✔	✔	✔
Wrestling	✔	✔	✔	✔	✔	✔	✔	✔	✔	✔	✔

WEIGHT TRAINING EXERCISES FOR MACHINES AND FREE WEIGHTS

Body Part	Nautilus	Universal Gym	Free Weights
Neck	4-way neck	Neck-conditioning station	Neck harness Manual exercises
Trapezius ("Traps")	Overhead press Lateral raise Reverse pullover Compound row Shoulder shrug Rowing back	Shoulder press Shoulder shrug Upright row Bent-over row Front raise Pull-up	Overhead press Lateral raise Shoulder shrug Power clean Upright row
Deltoids	Lateral raise Overhead press Reverse pullover Double chest 10° chest 50° chest Seated dip Bench press Compound row Rotary shoulder	Bench press Shoulder shrug Shoulder press Upright row Front raise Pull-up	Raise Bench press Shoulder press Upright row Pull-up
Biceps	Biceps curl Lat pull	Biceps curl Lat pull	Biceps curl Lat pull Pull-up
Triceps	Triceps extension Seated dip Triceps exten. (lat machine) Bench press Overhead press	French curl Dip Triceps exten. (lat machine) Bench press Seated press	French curl Dip Triceps exten. (lat machine) Bench press Military press
Latissimus dorsi ("Lats")	Pullover Behind neck Torso arm Lat pull Seated dip Compound row	Pull-up Lat pull Bent-over row Pullover Dip	Pull-up Pullover Dip Bent-over row Lat pull
Abdominals	Abdominal Rotary torso	Hip flexor Leg raise Crunch Sit-up Side-bend	Hip flexor Leg raise Crunch Sit-up Side-bend Isometric tightener
Lower back	Lower back	Back extension Back leg raise	Back extension Good-morning

(Continued)

(Continued)

Body Part	Nautilus	Universal Gym	Free Weights
Thigh and buttocks	Leg press	Leg press	Squat
	Leg extension	Leg curls	Leg press
	Leg curl	Leg extension	Leg extension
	Hip adductor	Adductor kick	Leg curl
	Hip abductor	Abductor kick	Power clean
		Back hip extension	Snatch
			Dead lift
Calf	Seated calf	Calf press	Heel raise
	Heel raise: multiexercise		

APPENDIX 3

Norms and Test Procedures for Measuring Strength

NORMS FOR BODY COMPOSITION, PERCENT FAT

Percent fat can be calculated by many methods, including underwater weighing, skinfold, bioelectrical impedance, and ultrasound. *Source:* The Cooper Institute for Aerobics Research, Dallas, TX, 1995.

MEN	AGE (YEARS)				
Rating	*20–29*	*30–39*	*40–49*	*50–59*	*60+*
Very lean	5.2	9.1	11.4	12.9	13.1
Excellent	9.4	13.9	16.3	17.9	18.4
Good	14.1	17.5	19.6	21.3	22.0
Fair	17.4	20.5	22.5	24.1	25.0
Poor	22.4	24.2	26.1	27.5	28.5
Very poor	29.1	29.9	31.5	32.4	33.4

WOMEN	AGE (YEARS)				
Rating	*20–29*	*30–39*	*40–49*	*50–59*	*60+*
Very lean	10.8	13.4	16.1	18.8	16.8
Excellent	17.1	18.0	21.3	25.0	25.1
Good	20.6	21.6	24.9	28.5	29.3
Fair	23.7	24.9	28.1	31.6	32.5
Poor	27.7	29.3	32.1	35.6	36.6
Very poor	35.4	35.7	37.8	39.6	40.5

NORMS FOR 1-MINUTE SIT-UPS

Instructions: Determine the number of bent-knee sit-ups you can do in 1 minute, with feet held by spotter, and hands folded across the chest. *Source:* The Cooper Institute for Aerobics Research, Dallas, TX, 1995.

MEN	AGE (YEARS)					
Rating	*< 20*	*20–29*	*30–39*	*40–49*	*50–59*	*60+*
Superior	62	55	51	47	43	39
Excellent	51	47	43	39	35	30
Good	47	42	39	34	28	22
Fair	41	38	35	29	24	19
Poor	36	33	30	24	19	15
Very poor	27	27	23	17	12	7

WOMEN	AGE (YEARS)					
Rating	*< 20*	*20–29*	*30–39*	*40–49*	*50–59*	*60+*
Superior	55	51	42	38	30	28
Excellent	46	44	35	29	24	17
Good	36	38	29	24	20	11
Fair	32	32	25	20	14	6
Poor	28	27	20	14	10	3
Very poor	25	18	11	7	5	0

NORMS FOR 1 REPETITION MAXIMUM BENCH PRESS

(Bench-press ratio) *Source:* The Cooper Institute for Aerobics Research, Dallas, TX, 1995.

Instructions: Warm up. Determine the maximum weight you can bench-press for 1 repetition (universal dynamic variable resistance machine). Divide your max bench press (lb.) by your body weight (lb.) to determine your bench-press ratio.

MEN	AGE (YEARS)					
Rating	*< 20*	*20–29*	*30–39*	*40–49*	*50–59*	*60+*
Superior	1.76	1.63	1.35	1.20	1.05	0.94
Excellent	1.34	1.32	1.12	1.00	0.90	0.82
Good	1.19	1.14	0.98	0.88	0.79	0.72
Fair	1.06	0.99	0.88	0.80	0.71	0.66
Poor	0.89	0.88	0.78	0.72	0.63	0.57
Very poor	0.76	0.72	0.65	0.59	0.53	0.49

WOMEN	AGE (YEARS)					
Rating	*< 20*	*20–29*	*30–39*	*40–49*	*50–59*	*60+*
Superior	0.88	1.01	0.82	0.77	0.68	0.72
Excellent	0.77	0.80	0.70	0.62	0.55	0.54
Good	0.65	0.70	0.60	0.54	0.48	0.47
Fair	0.58	0.59	0.53	0.50	0.44	0.43
Poor	0.53	0.51	0.47	0.43	0.39	0.38
Very poor	0.41	0.44	0.39	0.35	0.31	0.26

NORMS FOR 1 REPETITION MAXIMUM LEG PRESS

(Leg-press ratio) *Source:* The Cooper Institute for Aerobics Research, Dallas, TX, 1995.

Instructions: Warm up. Determine the maximum weight you can leg-press on a Universal Gym for 1 repetition. Divide your max leg press (lb.) by your body weight (lb.) to determine your leg-press ratio.

MEN	AGE (YEARS)					
Rating	*< 20*	*20–29*	*30–39*	*40–49*	*50–59*	*60+*
Superior	2.82	2.40	2.20	2.02	1.90	1.80
Excellent	2.28	2.13	1.93	1.82	1.71	1.62
Good	2.04	1.97	1.77	1.68	1.58	1.49
Fair	1.90	1.83	1.65	1.57	1.46	1.38
Poor	1.70	1.63	1.52	1.44	1.32	1.25
Very poor	1.46	1.42	1.34	1.27	1.15	1.08

WOMEN	AGE (YEARS)					
Rating	*< 20*	*20–29*	*30–39*	*40–49*	*50–59*	*60+*
Superior	1.88	1.98	1.68	1.57	1.43	1.43
Excellent	1.71	1.68	1.47	1.37	1.25	1.18
Good	1.59	1.50	1.33	1.23	1.10	1.04
Fair	1.38	1.37	1.21	1.13	0.99	0.93
Poor	1.22	1.22	1.09	1.02	0.88	0.85
Very poor	1.06	0.99	0.96	0.85	0.72	0.63

NORMS FOR PUSH-UPS, MEN

Instructions: Assume push-up starting position by lying face down, body and arms straight, and weight supported on your toes and hands. Lower your body until your chest touches the floor, then push up to the starting position. Do as many push-ups as possible. *Source:* The Cooper Institute for Aerobics Research, Dallas, TX, 1995, and a survey of published sources.

	AGE (YEARS)					
Rating	*< 20*	*20–29*	*30–39*	*40–49*	*50–59*	*60+*
Superior	64	62	52	40	39	28
Excellent	49	47	39	30	25	23
Good	39	37	30	24	19	18
Fair	31	29	24	18	13	10
Poor	24	22	17	11	9	6
Very poor	15	13	9	5	3	2

NORMS FOR MODIFIED PUSH-UPS, WOMEN

Instructions: Assume push-up starting position by lying face down, body and arms straight, and weight supported on your knees and hands. Lower your body until your chest touches the floor, then push up to the starting position. Do as many push-ups as possible. *Source:* The Cooper Institute for Aerobics Research, Dallas, TX, 1995, and a survey of published sources.

	AGE (YEARS)					
Rating	*< 20*	*20–29*	*30–39*	*40–49*	*50–59*	*60+*
Superior	50	45	39	33	28	20
Excellent	41	36	31	24	21	15
Good	35	30	24	18	17	12
Fair	28	23	19	13	12	5
Poor	22	17	11	6	6	2
Very poor	14	9	4	1	0	0

NORMS FOR COMBINED RIGHT- AND LEFT-HAND GRIP STRENGTH

Instructions: Using a hand-grip dynamometer, measure your maximum grip strength for your left and right hands and combine the score (left hand + right hand). Make two measurements for each hand, measuring each alternately. Record your measurements in kilograms. From survey of published sources.

MEN	AGE (YEARS)					
Rating	*< 20*	*20–29*	*30–39*	*40–49*	*50–59*	*60+*
Superior	137	136	135	128	119	111
Excellent	121	120	120	117	108	99
Good	112	111	111	108	100	91
Fair	105	104	104	100	94	84
Poor	96	95	94	91	85	76
Very poor	82	81	81	76	74	62

WOMEN	AGE (YEARS)					
Rating	*< 20*	*20–29*	*30–39*	*40–49*	*50–59*	*60+*
Superior	78	78	76	74	72	67
Excellent	71	71	69	67	63	56
Good	63	63	61	59	54	51
Fair	58	58	56	54	50	47
Poor	53	53	51	49	47	45
Very poor	45	45	43	41	40	38

Fitness Norms from *The Physical Fitness Specialist Manual,* The Cooper Institute for Aerobics Research, Dallas, TX, revised 1996. Used with permission.

APPENDIX 4

Web Sites for Further Information

BASIC PRINCIPLES OF PHYSICAL FITNESS

American Alliance for Health, Physical Education, Recreation, and Dance (AAHPERD) A professional organization dedicated to promoting quality education programs to improve the health and fitness of Americans.
    800-213-7193
    http://www.aahperd.org

American College of Sports Medicine (ACSM) Provides brochures, publications, and audio- and videotapes on the positive effects of exercise.
    317-637-9200
    http://www.acsm.org/sportsmed

American Council on Exercise (ACE) Promotes exercise and fitness for all Americans; the Web site features fact sheets on many consumer topics, including choosing shoes, cross-training, steroids, and getting started on an exercise program.
    800-529-8227 (Consumer Fitness Hotline)
    http://www.acefitness.org

American Medical Association/Personal Trainer Includes a fitness assessment and guidelines for creating a safe, effective program for developing the health-related components of fitness.
    http://www.ama-assn.org/insight/gen_hlth/trainer

Balance Magazine An online health and fitness magazine with practical advice for exercisers.
    http://www.hyperlink.com/balance

Disabled Sports USA Provides sports and recreation services to people with physical or mobility disorders.
    301-217-0960
    http://www.nas.com/~dsusa

Fitness Management Magazine's Fitness World Includes current issues of the magazine, information about exercise books and videos, news highlights related to exercise, and answers to frequently asked questions.
    http://www.fitnessworld.com

The Fitness Partner Connection Jumpsite A resource of fitness-related information on the Internet.

http://primusweb.com/fitnesspartner

Fitness-Related Web Sites Includes many links to helpful fitness- and health-related sites.

http://www.montana.com/Stafford/fitnesslinks.html

Internet's Fitness Resource Provides extensive links to sites about general fitness, specific activities, and fitness equipment.

http://rampages.onramp.net/~chaz/index.html

Melpomene Institute Provides information about physical activity and health for women.

612-642-1951

http://www.melpomene.org

Physical Activity & Health Network Provides resources and links on the relationship between physical activity and health.

http://www.pitt.edu/~pahnet

Worldguide Online: Health and Fitness Forum Provides information on anatomy, cardiorespiratory endurance exercise, strength training, nutrition, and sports medicine.

http://www.worldguide.com/Fitness/hf.html

CARDIORESPIRATORY ENDURANCE

Aerobics and Fitness Association of America/Your Body Provides information on exercise, including how to choose an instructor, class, or facility; how to begin a walking program; and how to maintain an exercise program while traveling.

http://www.afaa.com/your_body/yourbody.html

American Heart Association Provides information on cardiovascular health and disease, including the role of exercise in maintaining heart health and exercise tips for people of all ages.

800-AHA-USA1

http://www.americanheart.org

Dr. Pribut's Running Injuries Page Provides information about running and many types of running injuries.

http://www.clark.net/pub/pribut/spsport.html

Exploratorium's Science of Cycling Describes different types of bikes and how muscles work to power a cycle.

http://www.exploratorium.edu/cycling

Franklin Institute Science Museum/The Heart: An Online Exploration An online museum exhibit with information on the structure and function of the heart, blood vessels, and respiratory system.

http://www.fi.edu/biosci/heart.html

Physician and Sportsmedicine Provides many articles with easy-to-understand advice about exercise injuries.
>   http://www.physsportsmed.com

Runner's World Online Contains a wide variety of information about running, including tips for beginning runners, advice about training, and a shoe buyer's guide.
>   http://www.runnersworld.com

Yahoo/Recreation Contains links to many sites with practical advice on many sports and activities.
>   http://www.yahoo.com/Recreation/Sports

MUSCULAR STRENGTH AND ENDURANCE

Biomechanics Worldwide A resource site with links to many other sites relating to biomechanics; topics include muscle mechanics and sports techniques.
>   http://www.per.ualberta.ca/biomechanics

Human Anatomy Online Provides text, illustrations, and animation about the muscular system, nerve-muscle connections, muscular contraction, and other topics.
>   http://www.innerbody.com/indexbody.html

National Strength and Conditioning Association Provides education and certification for professionals in strength and conditioning.
>   402-476-6669
>   http://www.nsca-cc.org

Nicholas Institute of Sports Medicine and Athletic Trauma Includes information on exercise physiology, physical therapy, sports medicine, and training.
>   http://www.nismat.org

University of California, San Diego/Muscle Physiology Home Page Provides an introduction to muscle physiology, including information about types of muscle fibers and energy cycles.
>   http://www.muscle.ucsd.edu

University of Michigan/Muscles in Action Interactive descriptions of muscle movements.
>   http://www.med.umich.edu/lrc/Hypermuscle/Hyper.html

FLEXIBILITY

Back Pain Prevention Tips for use at home, at work, and during exercise.
>   http://cst.lanl.gov/CST/backpain/mainback.html

FitnessLink/Stretching Exercises Information on a safe, effective stretching program.
>   http://www.fitnesslink.com/exercise/stretch.htm

NIH Back Pain Fact Sheet Provides basic information on the prevention and treatment of back pain.
http://www.ninds.nih.gov/HEALINFO/DISORDER/back%20pain/backpain.htm

Southern California Orthopedic Institute Provides information about a variety of orthopedic problems, including back injuries; also has illustrations of spinal anatomy.
http://www.scoi.com

Stretching and Flexibility: Everything You Never Wanted to Know Provides information about the physiology of stretching and different types of stretching exercises.
http://www.cs.huji.ac.il/papers/rma/stretching_toc.html

Body Composition

American Diabetes Association Provides information, a free newsletter, and referrals to local support groups; the Web site includes an online diabetes health-risk assessment.
http://www.diabetes.org

Healthy Body Calculator Calculates and evaluates BMI, body weight, and waist-to-hip ratio.
http://www.dietitian.com/ibw

National Heart, Lung, and Blood Institute Provides information on the latest federal obesity standards and a BMI calculator.
http://www.nhlbi.nih.gov/nhlbi/nhlbi.htm

National Institute of Diabetes and Digestive and Kidney Diseases Health Information/ Nutrition and Obesity Provides information about adult obesity: how it is defined and assessed, the risk factors associated with it, and its causes.
800-WIN-8090
http://www.niddk.nih.gov/health/nutrit/nutrit.htm

Shape Up America A site devoted to promoting healthy weight management; calculates and rates BMI and looks at why BMI is an important measure of health.
http://shapeup.org

Glossary

adaptation Changes in the body as a result of a biological stressor. For example, forcing muscles to contract against increased resistance causes them to increase in size.

aerobics Exercises that increase oxygen consumption, such as running or swimming, and improve respiratory and circulatory function.

American College of Sports Medicine The principal interdisciplinary organization of sports-medicine professionals. Represented disciplines include medicine, athletic training, exercise physiology, physical therapy, psychology, motor learning (study of how physical skills are learned), biomechanics (study of motion), chiropractic, and education.

amino acids Substances that form the principal components of proteins. They are taken in supplement form by some people to enhance muscle growth, but there is no evidence that they are effective.

anabolic steroids Synthetic male hormones taken by people to enhance athletic performance and body composition. (Anabolic: biochemical building processes.)

androgens Hormones that promote male sexual characteristics and cell protein synthesis. They are produced in the male testes and in the adrenal glands of both sexes.

androstenedione One of several hormones produced by the adrenal glands that is broken down to form testosterone. It is used as a muscle-building agent by some athletes but has many of the same side effects as anabolic steroids. Its use as a supplement is banned by most sports organizations.

anorexia athletica An eating disorder related to anorexia nervosa. People with this condition include excessive exercise as part of their obsessive preoccupation with body weight.

anorexia nervosa   An eating disorder characterized by a neurotic fixation on body fat and food.

atrophy   Decrease in size of a body part or tissue.

balanced diet   A diet composed of the basic six food groups: dairy products, protein foods, fruits, vegetables, whole-grain products, and fats.

body building   A form of weight training dedicated to improving the shape and appearance of the body.

bulimia   An eating disorder characterized by binge eating followed by forced vomiting.

carbohydrate   Organic compounds, such as sugars and starches, composed of carbon, hydrogen, and oxygen.

circuit training   A technique involving a series of weight-training stations. The weight trainer performs an exercise and rapidly moves to the next station with little or no rest. Circuit training develops cardiovascular endurance, though not as effectively as endurance exercises such as running, cycling, or swimming.

collar   Device that secures weights to barbells or dumbbells.

concentric muscle contraction   Application of force as the muscle shortens.

constant resistance   A form of weight training that uses a constant load, such as a barbell or dumbbell.

constant set method   Same weight and number of sets and repetitions are used for each exercise.

cool-down   A light exercise program done at the end of a workout to gradually return the body to its normal resting state.

coronary artery disease   A disease of the large arteries supplying the heart, sometimes called hardening of the arteries.

cycle training   A training technique that varies the type, volume, rest intervals, and intensity of workouts throughout the year. Also called "periodization of training."

dead-lift grip   Gripping the bar with one palm toward you and one away; sometimes called "mixed grip."

dehydroepiandrosterone (DHEA)   One of several hormones produced by the adrenal glands that is broken down to form testosterone. It is used as a muscle-building agent by some athletes but has many of the same side effects as anabolic steroids. Its use as a supplement is banned by most sports organizations.

eccentric loading   Loading the muscle while it is lengthening; sometimes called "negatives."

eccentric muscle contraction   Application of force as the muscle lengthens.

electrical muscle stimulation   Application of an electrical current to the skin over a muscle group for the purpose of contracting the muscle.

endurance   The ability to sustain a specific exercise intensity.

ergogenic aid   A substance or technique used to improve performance.

exercise physiology   The study of physiological function during exercise.

failure method   Doing an exercise to the point of fatigue.

fat-free weight   Lean body mass.

frequency   The number of training sessions per week.

giant sets   Use of multiple exercises in succession for the same muscle group.

glycogen   A complex carbohydrate stored principally in the liver and skeletal muscle. It is an extremely important fuel during most forms of exercise.

hyperplasia   Increase in the number of muscle cells (fibers).

hypertrophy   Increase in the size of a muscle fiber. Hypertrophy is usually stimulated by muscular overload.

intensity   The relative effort expended during an exercise; also, the amount of resistance or weight used.

isokinetic   Application of a force at a constant speed. A form of isotonic exercise.

isometric   Application of force without movement. Also called "static."

isotonic   Application of force resulting in movement. Also called "dynamic."

joint   Place where bones intersect. Joints are often surrounded by joint capsules and are supported by ligaments and, to a lesser degree, by muscles.

ligaments   Structures that connect bone to bone.

load   The intensity of exercise — that is, the weight or resistance used.

maximum lift   The maximum amount of weight you can lift in one repetition of an exercise.

medicine ball   A heavy ball usually weighing 1–20 pounds and made of leather, rubber, or plastic. Some medicine balls have handles.

motor unit   A motor nerve (nerve that initiates movement) connected to one or more muscle fibers.

motor unit recruitment   Activation of motor units by the central nervous system to exert force.

multipennate muscle   A muscle in which the fibers are aligned in several directions.

muscle definition   Property where size and shape of a muscle is clearly visible. Best developed by decreasing surface fat and increasing muscle size.

osteoporosis   A disease characterized by bone demineralization that is most common in postmenopausal women.

overload   To subject the body to more than normal stress.

overtraining   A condition caused by training too much or too intensely and not providing enough time to recover adequately. Symptoms include lack of energy, decreased physical performance, fatigue, depression, aching muscles and joints, and proneness to injury.

parallel   A squat position where the long axis of the thigh is parallel to the ground (i.e., a parallel squat).

peak power   The maximum value for work/time. Practically speaking, the maximum combination of weight (amount of weight on the bar) and speed (time it takes to lift the weight). Most people are capable of generating peak power in a particular lift at a weight that is 60 percent of the weight they can lift for one repetition.

periodization of training   A training technique that varies the volume and intensity of exercises between workouts. Also called "cycle training."

plyometrics   Rapid stretching of a muscle group that is undergoing eccentric stress (i.e., the muscle is exerting force while it lengthens) followed by a rapid concentric contraction. Sometimes called "implosion training."

power   In physics, power equals work per unit of time. In weight training, power is usually defined as the ability to exert force rapidly.

power rack   A device used to restrict the range of motion during an exercise.

pronated grip   Gripping the bar with palms away from you.

pyramiding   A training technique that uses increasing amounts of weight with succeeding sets. After a maximum weight is reached, the remaining sets are done with decreasing amounts of weight.

rack   A structure that holds or supports barbells. Racks are often used in squats, bench presses, incline presses, and preacher curls.

rehabilitation   The restoration of normal function through the use of therapeutic exercise and modalities.

repetition   The number of times an exercise is done during 1 set.

resistance   A measure of force that must be exerted by the muscles to perform an exercise.

rest   The period of time between exercises, sets of exercises, or workouts.

reversibility   Decrease in fitness caused by lack of training or injury.

set   A group of repetitions followed by rest.

speed loading   Moving a load as rapidly as possible.

sports medicine   A branch of medicine dealing with medical problems of athletes. Disciplines often considered part of sports medicine include exercise physiology, athletic training, biomechanics (study of motion), sports physical therapy, kinesiology, sports psychology, motor learning (study of how physical skills are learned), and sports chiropractic.

spot   To assist with an exercise. The spotter's main job is to help the lifter with the weight if the exercise can't be completed.

spot reducing   Reducing fat in a specific part of the body, such as the abdomen, legs, or hips. There is no evidence that spot reducing is possible. Except for plastic surgery (liposuction), it appears that body fat can be lost only by inducing a negative energy balance—expending more energy than taken in.

strength   The ability to exert force.

strength–speed sport   A sport that requires rapid, powerful movements. Examples include softball, soccer, tennis, alpine skiing, and field hockey.

stress   In weight training, stress is the resistance placed on muscles and joints during an exercise.

super sets   Two sets of exercises performed in rapid succession, usually working opposing muscle groups.

supinated grip   Gripping the bar with palms toward you.

tendons   Rigid structures that connect muscles to bones.

testosterone   The principal male hormone (androgen). It is produced by the testes, is responsible for the development of secondary sexual characteristics, and plays a role in muscle hypertrophy. (The principal androgen in women is androstenedione, produced by the adrenal glands.)

variable resistance   The imposition of variable loading during an exercise. Resistance is generally increased toward the end of the range of motion. Usually, you must use weight machines to do variable resistance exercises.

vitamins   A general term used to describe a group of organic substances, required in small amounts, that are essential to metabolism.

volume   The number of sets and repetitions in a workout.

warm-up   Low-intensity exercise done before full-effort physical activity in order to improve muscle and joint performance, prevent injury, reinforce motor skills, and maximize blood flow to the muscles and heart. In weight training, people often warm up by lifting lighter weights before attempting heavy weights.

weight-lifting belt   A belt, approximately 4 inches wide, used to support the abdomen and back and maintain proper spinal alignment during weight-lifting exercises.

wraps   Joint supports made of elastic bandages, neoprene, or leather.

References

Aagaard, P., and J. L. Andersen. 1998. "Correlation between contractile strength and myosin heavy-chain isoform composition in human skeletal muscle." *Med. Sci. Sports Exerc.* 30: 1217–1222.

"ACSM position stand on the recommended quantity and quality of exercise for developing and maintaining cardiorespiratory and muscular fitness, and flexibility in adults." 1998. *Med. Sci. Sports Exerc.* 30: 975–991.

American College of Sports Medicine. 1995. *ACSM's Guidelines for Exercise Testing and Prescription.* 5th ed. Baltimore: Williams and Wilkins.

American Medical Association, Council on Scientific Affairs. 1990. "Medical and non-medical uses of anabolic-androgenic steroids." *J. Amer. Med. Assoc.* 264: 2923–2927.

Appleby, M., M. Fisher, and M. Martin. 1994. "Myocardial infarction, hyperkalaemia and ventricular tachycardia in a young male body-builder." *Int. J. Cardiol.* 44: 171–174.

Armstrong, R. B., G. L. Warren, and J. A. Warren. 1991. "Mechanisms of exercise-induced muscle fibre injury." *Sports Med.* 12: 184–207.

Bahrke, M. S., C. E. Yesalosk, and J. E. Wright. 1990. "Psychological and behavioural effects of endogenous testosterone levels and anabolic-androgenic steroids among males: A review." *Sports Med.* 10: 303–337.

Beltz, S. D., and P. L. Doering. 1993. "Efficacy of nutritional supplements used by athletes." *Clin. Pharm.* 12: 900–908.

Berger, R. 1962. "Optimum repetitions for the development of strength." *Res. Quart. Am. Alliance Health Phys. Educ. Recrea.* 33: 334–338.

Berger, R. 1963. "Comparative effects of three weight training programs." *Res. Quart. Am. Alliance Health Phys. Educ. Recrea.* 34: 396–398.

Bergstrom, J., L. Hermansen, E. Hultman, and B. Saltin. 1967. "Diet, muscle glycogen and physical performance." *Acta Physiol. Scand.* 71: 140–150.

Blackburn, J. R., and M. C. Morrissey. 1998. "The relationship between open and closed kinetic chain strength of the lower limb and jumping performance." *J. Orthop. Sports Ther.* 27: 430–435.

Bobbert, M. F. 1990. "Drop jumping as a training method for jumping ability." *Sports Med.* 9: 7–22.

Bobbert, M. F., P. A. Huijing, and G. J. van Ingen Schenau. 1987. "Drop jumping. I. The influence of jumping technique on the biomechanics of jumping." *Med. Sci. Sports Exer.* 19: 332–338.

Booth, F. W., and D. B. Thomason. 1991. "Molecular and cellular adaptation of muscle in response to exercise: Perspectives of various models." *Physiol. Rev.* 71: 541–585.

Brooks, G. A. 1987. "Amino acid and protein metabolism during exercise and recovery." *Med. Sci. Sports Exer.* 19 (Suppl.): 150–156.

Brooks, G. A., and T. D. Fahey. 1987. *Fundamentals of Human Performance.* New York: Macmillan.

Brooks, G. A., T. D. Fahey, and T. White. 1996. *Exercise Physiology: Human Bioenergetics and Its Applications.* 2d ed. Mountain View, CA: Mayfield.

Brown, C. H., and J. H. Wilmore. 1974. "The effects of maximal resistance training on the strength and body composition of women athletes." *Med. Sci. Sports* 6: 174–177.

Brown, R. D., and J. M. Harrison. 1986. "The effects of a strength training program on the strength and self-concept of two female age groups." *Res. Quart. Sport Exer.* 57: 315–320.

Buckley, W. E., C. E. Yasalis, K. E. Friedl, W. A. Anderson, A. L. Streit, and J. E. Wright. 1988. "Estimated prevalence of anabolic steroid use among male high school seniors." *J. Amer. Med. Assoc.* 260: 3441–3445.

Butterfield, G., and D. Calloway. 1984. "Physical activity improves protein utilization in young men." *Br. J. Nutr.* 51: 171–184.

Caiozzo V. J., F. Haddad, M. J. Baker, and K. M. Baldwin. 1996. "Influence of mechanical loading on myosin heavy-chain protein and mRNA isoform expression." *J. Appl. Physiol.* 80: 1503–1512.

Carpinelli, R. N., and R. M. Otto. 1998. "Strength training: Single versus multiple sets." *Sports Med.* 26: 73–84.

Cartana, J., T. Segues, M. Yebras, N. J. Rothwell, and M. J. Stock. 1994. "Anabolic effects of clenbuterol after long-term treatment and withdrawal in the rat." *Metabolism* 43: 1086–1092.

Castro, M. J., D. J. McCann, J. D. Shaffrath, and W. C. Adams. 1995. "Peak torque per unit cross-sectional area differs between strength-trained and untrained young adults." *Med. Sci. Sports Exer.* 27: 397–403.

Celejowa, I., and M. Homa. 1970. "Food intake, nitrogen and energy balance in Polish weight lifters, during a training camp." *Nutr. and Met.* 12: 259–275.

Chilibeck, P. D., D. G. Sale, and C. E. Webber. 1995. "Exercise and bone mineral density." *Sports Med.* 19: 103–122.

Chu, D. 1994. *Jumping into Plyometrics.* Champaign, IL: Leisure Press.

Clarkson, P. M., and D. J. Newham. 1997. "Associations between muscle soreness, damage, and fatigue." *Adv. Exp. Med. Biol.* 384: 457–469.

Consolazio, C. F., H. L. Johnson, R. A. Dramise, and J. A. Skata. 1975. "Protein metabolism during intensive physical training in the young adult." *Am. J. Clin. Nutr.* 28: 29–35.

Costill, D. L., E. F. Coyle, W. F. Fink, G. R. Lesmes, and F. A. Witzmann. 1979. "Adaptations in skeletal muscle following strength training." *J. Appl. Physiol.* 46: 96–99.

Costill, D. L., and J. M. Miller. 1980. "Nutrition for endurance sport: Carbohydrate and fluid balance." *Int. J. Sports Med.* 1: 2–14.

Coyle, E. F., S. Bell, D. L. Costill, and W. J. Fink. 1978. "Skeletal muscle fiber characteristics of world class shot-putters." *Res. Quart.* 49: 278–284.

Darden, E. 1982. *The Nautilus Bodybuilding Book.* Chicago: Contemporary Books.

Darden, E. 1984. *The Nautilus Advanced Bodybuilding Book.* New York: Simon & Schuster.

Department of Health and Human Services. 1996. *Physical Activity and Health: A Report of the Surgeon General.* Atlanta: U.S. Department of Health and Human Services, Centers for Disease Control and Prevention, National Center for Chronic Disease Prevention and Health Promotion.

Fahey, T. D. 1987. *Athletic Training: Principles and Practice.* Mountain View, CA: Mayfield.

Fahey, T. D., L. Akka, and R. Rolph. 1975. "Body composition and $\dot{V}O_{2max}$ of exceptional weight-trained athletes." *J. Appl. Physiol.* 39: 559–561.

Fahey, T. D., and G. Hutchinson. 1992. *Weight Training for Women.* Mountain View, CA: Mayfield.

Fahey, T. D., P. M. Insel, and W. T. Roth. 1999. *Fit and Well.* 3d ed. Mountain View, CA: Mayfield.

Fahey, T. D., and M. S. Pearl. 1998. "The hormonal and perceptive effects of phosphatidylserine administration during two weeks of resistive exercise-induced overtraining." *Biol. Sport.* 15: 135–144.

Fleck, S. J., and W. J. Kraemer. 1997. *Designing Resistance Training Programs.* Champaign, IL: Human Kinetics.

Fowler, N. E., Z. Trzaskoma, A. Wit, L. Iskra, and A. Lees. 1995. "The effectiveness of a pendulum swing for the development of leg strength and counter-movement jump performance." *J. Sports Sci.* 13: 101–108.

Garfinkle, S., and E. Cafarelli. 1992. "Relative changes in maximal force, EMG, and muscle cross-sectional area after isometric training." *Med. Sci. Sports Exerc.* 24: 1220–1227.

Garhammer, J. 1980. "Power production by Olympic weightlifters." *Med. Sci. Sports Exer.* 12: 54–60.

Garhammer, J. 1991. "A comparison of maximal power outputs between elite male and female weightlifters in competition." *Int. J. Sport Biomech.* 7: 3–11.

Goldberg, A. L. 1972. "Mechanisms of growth and atrophy of skeletal muscle." In R. G. Cassens, ed., *Muscle Biology.* New York: Marcel Dekker.

Gollnick, P. D., R. B. Armstrong, C. W. Saubertt, K. Piehl, and B. Saltin. 1972. "Enzyme activity and fiber composition in skeletal muscle of trained and untrained men." *J. Appl. Physiol.* 33: 312–319.

Gonyea, W. J., and D. Sale. 1982. "Physiology of weight lifting." *Arch. Phys. Med. Rehabil.* 63: 235–237.

Hakkinen, K., A. Pakarinen, and M. Kallinen. 1992. "Neuromuscular adaptations and serum hormones in women during short-term intensive strength training." *Eur. J. Appl. Physiol.* 64: 106–111.

Harridge, S. D., R. Bottinelli, M. Canepari, M. Pellegrino, C. Reggiani, M. Esbjornsson, P. D. Balsom, and B. Saltin. 1998. "Sprint training, *in vitro* and *in vivo* muscle function, and myosin heavy-chain expression." *J. Appl. Physiol.* 84: 442–449.

Hickson, R. C. 1980. "Interference of strength development by simultaneously training for strength and endurance." *Eur. J. Appl. Physiol.* 45: 255–263.

Higbie, E. J., K. J. Cureton, G. L. Warren 3d, and B. M. Prior. 1996. "Effects of concentric and eccentric training on muscle strength, cross-sectional area, and neural activation." *J. Appl. Physiol.* 81: 2173–2181.

Hill, A. V. 1970. *First and Last Experiments in Muscle Mechanics.* Cambridge: Cambridge University Press.

Hortobagyi, T., J. P. Hill, J. A. Houmard, D. D. Fraser, N. J. Lambert, and R. G. Israel. 1996. "Adaptive responses to muscle lengthening and shortening in humans." *J. Appl. Physiol.* 80: 765–772.

Huie, M. J. 1994. "An acute myocardial infarction occurring in an anabolic steroid user." *Med. Sci. Sports Exer.* 26: 408–413.

Karlsson, J., and B. Saltin. 1971. "Diet, muscle glycogen and endurance performance." *J. Appl. Physiol.* 31: 203–206.

Kawakami, Y., T. Abe, and T. Fukunaga. 1993. "Muscle-fiber pennation angles are greater in hypertrophied than in normal muscles." *J. Appl. Physiol.* 74: 2740–2744.

Kelley, G. 1996. "Mechanical overload and skeletal muscle fiber hyperplasia: A meta-analysis." *J. Appl. Physiol.* 81: 1584–1588.

King, A. C., and D. L. Tribble. 1981. "The role of exercise in weight regulation in nonathletes." *Sports Med.* 11: 331–349.

Kleiber, M. 1961. *The Fire of Life.* New York: Wiley & Sons.

Komi, P. V., ed. 1992. *Strength and Power in Sport.* London: Blackwell Scientific Publications.

Kraemer, W. J. 1988. "Endocrine responses to resistance exercise." *Med. Sci. Sports Exer.* 20 (Suppl.): 152–157.

Kraemer, W. J., J. F. Patton, S. E. Gordon, E. A. Harman, M. R. Deschenes, K. Reynolds, R. U. Newton, N. T. Triplett, and J. E. Dziados. 1995. "Compatibility of high-intensity strength and endurance training on hormonal and skeletal muscle adaptations." *J. Appl. Physiol.* 78: 976–989.

Kuramoto, A. K., and V. G. Payne. 1995. "Predicting muscular strength in women: A preliminary study." *Res. Q. Exer. Sport* 66: 168–172.

Lemon, P. W. R. 1987. "Protein and exercise." *Med. Sci. Sports Exer.* 19 (Suppl.): 179–190.

Lesmes, G. R., D. Costill, E. F. Coyle, and W. J. Fink. 1978. "Muscle strength and power changes during maximal isokinetic training." *Med. Sci. Sports* 10: 266–269.

Linderman, J., T. D. Fahey, L. Kirk, J. Musselman, and B. Dolinar. 1992. "The effects of sodium bicarbonate and pyridoxine-alpha-ketoglutarate on short-term maximal exercise capacity." *J. Sports Sci.* 10: 243–253.

MacDougall, J. D., G. R. Ward, D. G. Sale, and J. R. Sutton. 1977. "Biochemical adaptation of human skeletal muscle to heavy resistance training and immobilization." *J. Appl. Physiol.* 43: 700–703.

MacIntyre, D. L., W. D. Reid, and D. C. McKenzie. 1995. "Delayed muscle soreness. The inflammatory response to muscle injury and its clinical implications." *Sports Med.* 20: 24–40.

Manning, R. J., J. E. Graves, D. M. Carpenter, S. H. Leggett, and M. L. Pollock. 1990. "Constant vs. variable resistance knee extension training." *Med. Sci. Sports Exer.* 22: 397–401.

Mastropaolo, J. A. 1992. "A test of the maximum-power theory for strength." *Eur. J. Appl. Physiol.* 65: 415–420.

Maugham, R. J., J. S. Watson, and J. Weir. 1983. "Relationship between muscle strength and muscle cross-sectional area in male sprinters and endurance runners." *Eur. J. Appl. Physiol.* 50: 309–318.

McCall, G. E., W. C. Byrnes, A. Dickinson, P. M. Pattany, and S. J. Fleck. 1996. "Muscle fiber hypertrophy, hyperplasia, and capillary density in college men after resistance training." *J. Appl. Physiol.* 81: 2004–2012.

McCarthy, J. P., J. C. Agre, B. K. Graf, M. A. Pozniak, and A. C. Vailas. 1995. "Compatibility of adaptive responses with combining strength and endurance training." *Med. Sci. Sports Exer.* 27: 429–436.

McCarthy, N., A. L. Hicks, J. Martin, and C. E. Webber. 1995. "Long-term resistance training in the elderly: Effects on dynamic strength, exercise capacity, muscle, and bone." *J. Gerontol. A. Biol. Sci. Med. Sci.* 50: B97–104.

McDonagh, M. J. N., and C. T. Davis. 1984. "Adaptive response of mammalian skeletal muscle to exercise with high loads." *Eur. J. Appl. Physiol.* 52: 139–155.

Moritani, T., and H. A. deVries. 1979. "Neural factors versus hypertrophy in the time course of muscle strength gain." *Amer. J. Phys. Med.* 58: 115–130.

Nardone, A., C. Romano, and M. Schieppatgi. 1989. "Selective recruitment of high-threshold human motor units during voluntary isotonic lengthening of active muscles." *J. Physiol.* 409: 451–471.

Peterson, G. E., and T. D. Fahey. 1984. "HDL-C in five elite athletes using anabolic-androgenic steroids." *Physician Sportsmed.* 12(6): 120–130.

Phillips, C. A. 1991. *Functional Electrical Rehabilitation.* New York: Springer-Verlag.

Pope, H. G., and D. L. Katz. 1988. "Affective disorders and psychotic symptoms associated with anabolic steroids." *Amer. J. Psychiatry* 145: 487–490.

Pope, H. G., and D. L. Katz. 1994. "Psychiatric and medical effects of anabolic-androgenic steroid use. A controlled study of 160 athletes." *Arch. Gen. Psychiatry* 51: 375–382.

Rogozkin, V. 1988. *Metabolism of Anabolic Androgenic Steroids.* St. Petersburg, Russia: Hayka.

Rooney, K. J., R. D. Herbert, and R. J. Balnave. 1994. "Fatigue contributes to the strength training stimulus." *Med. Sci. Sports Exer.* 26: 1160–1164.

Sale, D. G. 1988. "Neural adaptation to resistance training." *Med. Sci. Sports Exer.* 20 (Suppl.): 135–145.

Saltin, B., and P. D. Gollnick. 1983. "Skeletal muscle adaptability: Significance for metabolism and performance." In *Handbook of Physiology. Skeletal Muscle.* Bethesda, MD: Am. Physiol. Soc., sect. 10, ch. 19, pp. 555–631.

Shangold, M., and G. Merkin, eds. 1994. *Women and Exercise: Physiology and Sports Medicine.* 2d ed. Philadelphia: F. A. Davis.

Shephard, R. J., E. Bouhlel, H. Vandewalle, and H. Monod. 1988. "Muscle mass as a factor limiting physical work." *J. Appl. Physiol.* 64: 1472–1479.

Soest, A. J. van, and M. F. Bobbert. 1993. "The role of muscle properties in control of explosive movements." *Biol. Cybern.* 69: 195–204.

Starson, R. S., F. C. Hagerman, and R. S. Hikida. 1981. "The effects of detraining on an elite power lifter." *J. Neuro. Sci.* 51: 247–257.

Sugden, P. H., and S. J. Fuller. 1991. "Regulation of protein turnover in skeletal and cardiac muscle." *Biochem. J.* 273: 21–37.

Taaffe, D. R., L. Pruitt, J. Reim, G. Butterfield, and R. Marcus. 1995. "Effect of sustained resistance training on basal metabolic rate in older women." *J. Am. Geriatr. Soc.* 43: 465–471.

Tamaki, T., T. Sekine, A. Akatsuka, S. Uchiyama, and S. Nakano. 1992. "Detection of neuromuscular junctions on isolated branched muscle fibers: Application of nitric acid fiber digestion method for scanning electron microscopy." *J. Electron Microsc.* 41: 76–81.

Tamaki, T., S. Uchiyama, and S. Nakano. 1992. "A weight-lifting exercise model for inducing hypertrophy in the hindlimb muscles of rats." *Med. Sci. Sports Exer.* 24: 881–886.

Tennant, F., D. L. Black, and R. O. Voy. 1988. "Anabolic steroid dependence with opioid features." *New Eng. J. Med.* 319: 578.

Tesch, P. A., and L. Larsson. 1982. "Muscle hypertrophy in bodybuilders." *Eur. J. Appl. Physiol.* 49: 301–306.

Thomis, M. A. I., G. P. Beunen, H. H. Maes, C. J. Blimkie, M. Van Leemputte, A. L. Claessens, G. Marchal, E. Willems, and R. F. Vlietinck. 1998. "Strength training: Importance of genetic factors." *Med. Sci. Sports Exerc.* 30: 724–731.

Thorstensson, A. 1976. "Muscle strength, fibre types and enzyme activities in man." *Acta Physiol. Scand.* (Suppl.) 443: 1–45.

Torgan, C. E., G. J. Etgen, J. T. Brozinick, R. E. Wilcos, and J. L. Ivy. 1993. "Interaction of aerobic exercise training and clenbuterol: Effects on insulin-resistant muscle." *J. Appl. Physiol.* 75: 1471–1476.

Treuth, M. S., G. R. Hunter, T. Kekes-Szabo, R. L. Weinsier, M. I. Goran, and L. Berland. 1995. "Reduction in intra-abdominal adipose tissue after strength training in older women." *J. Appl. Physiol.* 78: 1425–1431.

Walberg, J. L. 1989. "Aerobic exercise and resistance weight-training during weight reduction." *Sports Med.* 47: 343–356.

Welbergen E., H. C. G. Kemper, J. J. Knibbe, H. M. Toussaint, and L. Clijsen. 1991. "Efficiency and effectiveness of stoop and squat lifting at different frequencies." *Ergonomics* 34: 613–624.

Welle, S., C. Thornton, and M. Statt. 1995. "Myofibrillar protein synthesis in young and old human subjects after three months of resistance training." *Am. J. Physiol.* 268: E422–427.

Williams, M. H. 1994. "The use of nutritional ergogenic aids in sports: Is it an ethical issue?" *Int. J. Sports Nutr.* 4: 120–131.

Williams, P. E., T. Cantanese, E. G. Lucey, and G. Goldspink. 1988. "The importance of stretch and contractile activity in the prevention of connective tissue accumulation in muscle." *J. Anat.* 158: 109–114.

Wilson, G. J., A. J. Murphy, and A. Walshe. 1996. "The specificity of strength training: The effect of posture." *Eur. J. Appl. Physiol.* 73: 346–352.

Wright, J. 1980. "Anabolic steroids and athletics." *Exer. and Sports Sci. Rev.* 8: 149–202.

Index